Robert R. Carkhuff, Ph.D.

The
Human Sciences

Volume IV
Interpersonal Skills and
Human Productivity

Published by: HRD Press, Inc.
                 22 Amherst Road
                 Amherst, MA 01002
                 800-822-2801 (U.S. and Canada)
                 413-253-3488
                 413-253-3490 (fax)

ISBN 978-1-61014-300-4

Editorial services by Robert W. Carkhuff
Graphics and production by Jean S. Miller
Cover design by Eileen Klockars
Promotion by Swift Global Media

The Human Sciences:
Volume IV. Interpersonal Skills and Human Productivity

Contents

1. **Introduction**... 1

2. **Interpersonal Models** 3
   Processing Model 3
   Living Skills.. 4
   Learning Skills.. 5
   Working Skills 6

3. **IPS Model Variations**.. 9
   Living Skills.. 9
   Learning Skills.. 9
   Working Skills 10

4. **Intervention Design**.. 13

5. **Mega-Research Design** 17

6. **The Effects of Interveners upon Recipients** 21
   Living Outcomes... 21
   Learning Outcomes 33
   Working Outcomes... 55

7. **The Effects of the Direct Training of Recipients** 67
   Living Outcomes... 67
   Learning Outcomes 80
   Working Outcomes... 89

8. **Summary and Overview**... 103
   Summary 103
   Processing Skills... 104
   Intervention Issues 109

9. **Conclusions and Implications**.. 113
   Living... 113
   Learning... 115
   Working.. 117

10. Human Processing and Human Productivity 121
    Sources of Economic Growth 121
    Sources of Human and Information Capital Development 125
    Toward Human Processing and Human Productivity 127
    Toward Personal Growth 130

References 133

About the Author

Among the most-cited scientists of the 20th century and already the most prolific in the 21st century, Robert R. Carkhuff is the author of *The Human Sciences.* His full biography and body of work may be viewed on his websites:

www.carkhuff.com

www.mcleanproject.com

www.carkhuffgenerativitylibrary.com

Carkhuff boldly confronts our current socioeconomic crisis:

"Generativity is the solution!"

"What is the question?"

1 Introduction

We are in a period of transition between the Industrial and Information Eras. In practice, it is more like a period of fragmentation (Aspy, Aspy and Roebuck, 1982; Carkhuff, 1983b; Cox, 1982; Naisbett, 1982). All of our socioeconomic, political, and educational institutions lag behind the demands made by the Information Age.

In the greater social context, the Information Age emphasizes data resources while our industrial mentalities continue to think in terms of capital. Similarly, our national economies perseverate in the face of the "global village" fashioned by our computer and telecommunication industries. The need for decentralization demanded by local databases is undermined by increasingly totalitarian attempts to centralize organizations, industries, and countries. Politics continue to be partisan in the face of increasingly enlightened citizens disposed to the issues of their own unique time and place. In summary, there is not only a great deal of foot-dragging by our leaders upon entering the Information Age, there is also an intensified reactionary effort to restore things as they were in the past.

We can see the fragmentation most clearly in the industrial context where manufacturing has been replaced by the so-called high technology industries, yet the vestiges of the past resource-based and protectionistic thinking linger. In this regard, the production of goods to meet human survival and comfort needs continues to dominate the need to *market* in order to provide services that help us to become more human. Short-term profits based on the immediate manipulation of the human condition retard the long-term profits based upon meeting and extending enduring human needs. Finally, resource-based thinking continues to hold back real productivity values, increasing results outputs while reducing resource inputs (Carkhuff, 1983b). In short, our industrial leaders have been on continuous and incremental reinforcement schedules; consequently, they are weak and impotent to do anything but ask us to dine at the last dinner of the dinosaurs.

1

The basic productivity systems themselves have changed in emphasis. Yet while human services are clearly in ascendancy over products as outputs, raw materials continue to dominate over information inputs; machinery supersedes the human mind of processing; and random sampling delays constant monitoring of results outputs and resource inputs as feedback. To sum, the productivity systems have not yet been dedicated to meeting human needs by maximizing results outputs and minimizing resource inputs.

In private and public sector organizations, leadership continues to be asserted by position rather than by the power of personal productivity. The organizations themselves are authoritarian and hierarchical while the greatest needs cry out for interdependency based on the complementary relationship of shared databases. The responsibilities continue to revolve around management rather than rely upon individual entrepreneurial initiative in little productivity centers throughout the organizations. Consequently, the relations are role-to-role rather than person-to-person and the dissemination of information is limited to the sparse data and response repertoires of a relatively few people. In short, the organizations remain the stolid, stone-age manifestations of Primitive Man rather than the dynamic, futuristic networking of truly Human Beings.

In turn, individuals have been retarded from becoming exemplary performers by continuing to emphasize their substantive specialties in single careers rather than developing core generic and supplementary skills in preparation for multiple careers. Relatedly, individual motives remain external-incentive-based rather than internal-actualization-based and their processing emphasizes conditioning rather than thinking. To summarize, our homes, schools, jobs, and communities continue to produce spinally conditioned, Industrial-Age performers rather than substantive informed thinkers.

In order to maximize the development of information, individuals and organizations are going to have to share data. The way that they share data is through the use of interpersonal skills. Each individual or unit or organization relates to the other individuals, units, or organizations by entering their frames of reference, seeing the world through their eyes, and communicating what they see. With this interpersonal communication, individual development and organizational dissemination is possible. Without it, neither is possible.

2 Interpersonal Models

Another way of characterizing the Information Era is in terms of interpersonal productivity. In order for individuals and organizations to become productive, they are going to have to process with productive purposes: they will dedicate their human mechanical processing to increasing beneficial resource outputs such as human services and products while reducing the investment of potentially detractive resource inputs such as raw materials drawn from finite natural resources.

There are a number of models of interpersonal skills. Most have failed to prove their effectiveness in terms of individual performance or organizational productivity. Experience-based encounter groups or sensitivity experiences are next to worthless. Behavioral social skills modeling and shaping programs offer limited goals and sources of learning. Didactic experiences teach facts and concepts but provide no kinesthetic skills-based learning experiences that enable us to file and retrieve permanent images in our temporal lobes. Only when all sources of learning—didactic, experiential, modeling, and shaping—are integrated and focused on specific interpersonal skills do we become productive individuals and organizations.

Processing Model

The basic model for interpersonal skills development is the Human Processing Skills (HPS) model (Carkhuff, 1969, 1983a, 1983b). As can be seen in Figure 1, the model is predicated upon phases of learning: the pre-learning phase in which the recipients are involved in the learning process; the initial phase (I) where the recipients explore where they are in relation to the learning experience; the transitional phase (II) where the recipients understand where they are in relation to where they want or need to be; and the final phase (III) where the recipients act to get from where they are to where they want or need to be. These phases are recycled by feedback from acting, which stimulates more extensive exploring, more accurate understanding, and more effective acting.

3

PHASES OF LEARNING

	I	II	III
LEARNERS:	EXPLORING →	UNDERSTANDING →	ACTING
	where they are in relation to learning experience	where they are in relation to where they want or need to be	to get from where they are to where they want or need to be

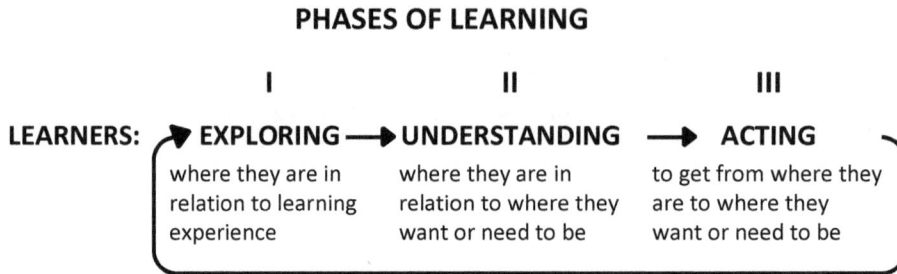

Figure 1. A Model for Human Processing

This human processing model may also be called the basic E-U-A model. All interpersonal facilitation skills models and technologies are built upon this basic model. These include helping models having to do with the living skills development and outcomes of different helpee populations. They also include the teaching-learning models facilitating learner or student skills development and outcomes. Finally, they include the working models expediting worker skills development and outcomes.

Living Skills

The recipients' movement through the phases of learning is guided by the helpers' interpersonal skills (IPS) (Carkhuff, 1969, 1983a, 1983b). As can be seen in Figure 2, the helpers attend, observe, and listen to the recipients in order to involve them in the learning process. The recipients give cues concerning their readiness to enter the exploration phase by attending to the experience without help.

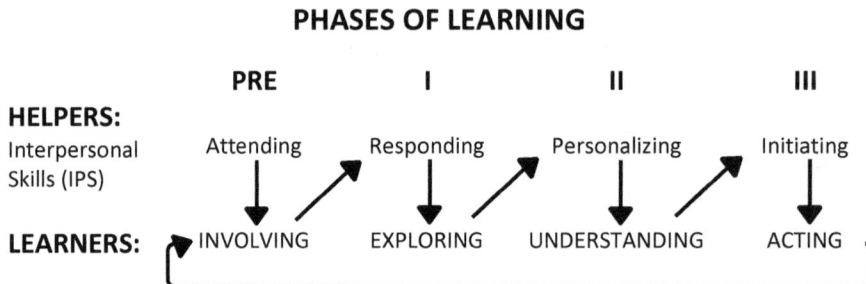

PHASES OF LEARNING

	PRE	I	II	III
HELPERS: Interpersonal Skills (IPS)	Attending	Responding	Personalizing	Initiating
LEARNERS:	INVOLVING	EXPLORING	UNDERSTANDING	ACTING

Figure 2. A Model for Living Skills Development

In turn, the helpers respond to the recipients by reflecting accurately the content, feeling, and meaning of the recipients' experience in order to facilitate their exploring where they are in relation to the experience. When the recipients emit cues concerning their ability to respond to their own experience, the helpers move forward to personalize the recipients' experience. The helpers personalize the meaning, problems, and goals of the recipients' experience in order to facilitate their understanding of their goals. Finally, when the recipients understand their own goals, the helpers initiate to help them act to achieve the goals. This is accomplished by defining the goals and developing the programs to achieve them. This IPS model may be seen as the basic helping model that facilitates living skills development. It applies to all instances of helping and human relationships, including especially child-rearing, teaching and training, counseling, and working relations.

Learning Skills

The recipients' movement through learning is also facilitated by Teaching Delivery Skills (TDS) (Carkhuff and Berenson, 1981). As can be seen in Figure 3, the teaching model is cumulative and developmental. The teachers or trainers employ teaching delivery skills to teach the content from the external frame of reference of the content and interpersonal skills to teach the learners from the learners' internal frames of reference. Thus, the teachers or trainers develop the skills content externally while attending to the learners internally in order to facilitate learner involvement during the pre-learning phase. During the initial phase of learning, the teachers diagnose the learners in terms of the external content while responding to the learners' frames of reference in order to facilitate learner exploration of experience. Transitionally, the teachers set goals in terms of the external diagnosis while personalizing the goals internally in order to facilitate learner understanding of goals. Finally, the teachers develop external programs to achieve the goals while initiating to individualize those programs internally in order to facilitate the learners acting to achieve goals. This IPS-based teaching model may be seen as the basic learning model that facilitates learning skills development. It applies to all instances of helping and human relations emphasizing teaching and training.

PHASES OF LEARNING

	PRE	I	II	III
TEACHERS:				
(IPS)	Attending	Responding	Personalizing	Initiating
	&	&	&	&
Teaching Delivery Skills (TDS)	Attending	Responding	Personalizing	Initiating
LEARNERS:	INVOLVING	EXPLORING	UNDERSTANDING	ACTING

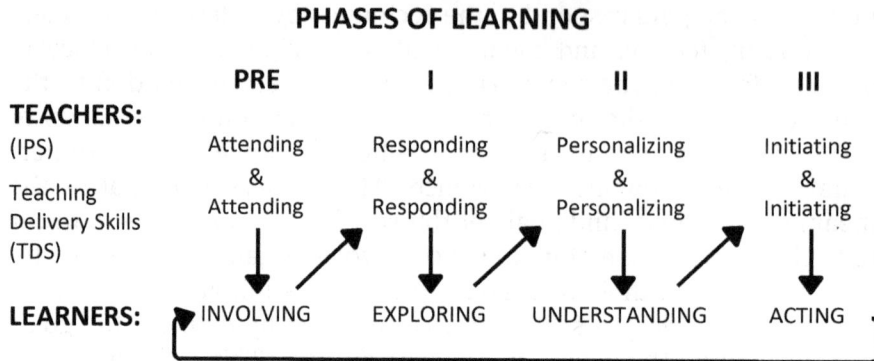

Figure 3. A Model for Learning Skills Development

Working Skills

The recipients' movement through learning is further facilitated by Working Delivery Skills (WDS) (Carkhuff and Friel, 1974). As can be seen in Figure 4, the working model is also cumulative and developmental. The employers or supervisors use working delivery skills to further complement the recipients' external efforts while addressing their internal experience. Thus, in the pre-learning phase, the employers integrate the work experience with the recipients' experience prior to engaging the recipients in task performance activities. During the initial phase of learning, the employers help to expand the alternative courses of action available to the recipients while responding to their experience of the alternatives. During the transitional phase, the employers help to narrow the recipients' courses to a preferred course of action while personalizing the recipients' experiences of that course of action. During the final phase of learning, the employers help to plan the tasks needed to implement the preferred courses while individualizing those tasks. This IPS-based model may be seen as the basic working model that facilitates working skills development. It applies to all instances of human relationships emphasizing task performance, problem solving, and goal achievement.

Interpersonal Models

PHASES OF LEARNING

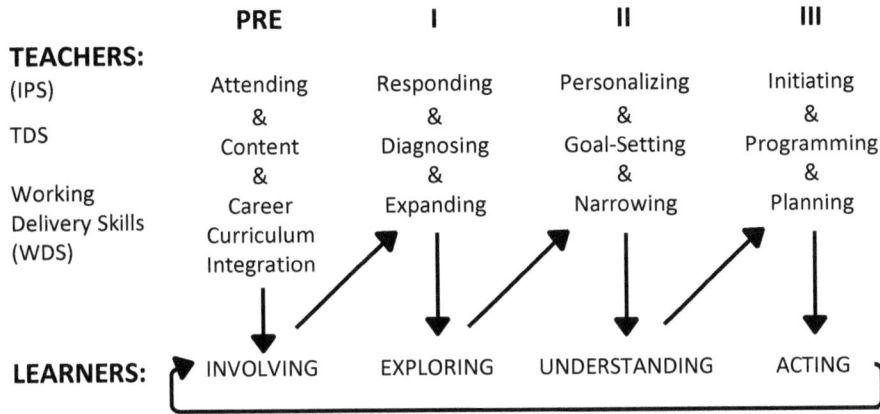

	PRE	**I**	**II**	**III**
TEACHERS:				
(IPS)	Attending	Responding	Personalizing	Initiating
	&	&	&	&
TDS	Content	Diagnosing	Goal-Setting	Programming
	&	&	&	&
Working	Career	Expanding	Narrowing	Planning
Delivery Skills	Curriculum			
(WDS)	Integration			
LEARNERS:	INVOLVING	EXPLORING	UNDERSTANDING	ACTING

Figure 4. A Model for Learning Skills Development

3 IPS Model Variations

There are many variations of the IPS-based models. Some have demonstrated a relationship with outcome. Others have not. These models also fall into the living, learning, and working categories.

Living Skills

The IPS-based models falling into this area are basically imitative of the original IPS model (Carkhuff, 1969, 1983a). Thus, for example, the works of Gazda (1973a) and Egan (1975) are direct restatements of the earlier work, emphasizing empathic responsiveness as the critical ingredient in facilitating client or helpee exploration. Kagan (1975), Ivey and Authier (1978), Authier and Gustafson (1973) and Danish and Hauer (1973) simply employ feedback methods emphasizing attending and responding skills that facilitate recipient involvement and exploration. In turn, Goldstein (1973) and his followers attempt to shape specific social-interpersonal action skills by structured learning therapy. All of these approaches, while presenting some evidence for effectively utilizing shaping methods, lack comprehensive and integrated E-U-A models for living effectiveness.

Learning Skills

Aspy and Roebuck (1977) have done the most work in the teaching-learning area. They have complemented the basic IPS teaching model with cognitive functioning categories. The cognitive categories emphasize a taxonomy of knowledge (Bloom, Englehart, Furst, Hill, and Krathwohl, 1956) and interaction analyses models focusing on analyses of the classroom interactions between teachers and learners (Flanders, 1970). Thus, in cognitive functioning, both teachers and learners may learn and demonstrate memory of facts or thinking to analyze a situation or solve a problem. Similarly, in interaction analyses, teacher expressions may serve to indirectly (accepting, praising, using, asking) or directly (lecturing, directing, criticizing) influence learner behavior while student talk may be analyzed as responsive to teacher initiations or initiated by the students. While these complementary cognitive and interaction analyses were helpful activities, Aspy and Roebuck (1977) found that their relationships to learner outcomes were dwarfed by those of the basic IPS-based teaching model. Today, Aspy and his associates emphasize the basic IPS model in all teacher and student training programs.

Working Skills

Pierce and others (1982; Carkhuff, 1983b) have developed the most distinctive work variation, the performance management system (PMS), based directly on the IPS model. Here the communication skills model emphasizes four distinct steps:

1. **Get** the other person's input, perspective, or point of view concerning the task to be performed.

2. **Give** your perspective of the task in a way the other person can hear and see.

3. **Merge** similar and dissimilar perspectives into a preferred solution.

4. **Go** through the steps required to reach the mutually-agreed-upon goal.

The "Get-Give-Merge and Go" (GGMG) model guides the supervisor through a three-step Problem-Reason-Direction (PRD) process that is designed to encourage employee participation in the identification and solution of specific performance problems:

1. **Problems**—identify performance problems in daily work settings.

2. **Reasons**—determine whether the reasons for the performance problems are under the influence of the environment or the employee.

3. **Directions**—develop a direction that will eliminate each reason and solve the performance problem.

The **GGMG-PRD** models have demonstrated extensive evidence for supervisor effectiveness in all phases of performance improvement and management. They offer vehicles to be integrated with other task-related functions, including performance appraisal, employee development, and merit compensation.

In summary, the IPS-based models have dominated the literature of interpersonal productivity for two decades. While there are variations of the IPS theme, all models emphasize responding to facilitate recipient exploring of the learning experience. All comprehensive IPS models emphasize personalizing to facilitate understanding and initiating individualized programs to facilitate acting. In this context, these interpersonal skills appear to be the necessary but not sufficient conditions for all human endeavors.

In the pages ahead, you will read an extensive review of the literature of IPS-based programs. The living skills section will emphasize the IPS-based helping skills models exclusively. The learning skills sections will emphasize the IPS-based teaching models with special attention given to the Aspy and Roebuck demonstrations. The working skills sections will emphasize the IPS-based working models including the Pierce GGMG-PRD model demonstrations. Following the reviewing of the research, the implications for human resource development and human productivity will be considered.

4 Intervention Design

There is a great deal of confusion surrounding the issues of process and outcome in all types of human resource development (HRD) activities (Carkhuff, 1969, 1971a, 1983b; Paul and Lentz, 1977; Suchman, 1967). This is particularly true with regard to different helping and human relationships leading to living, learning, and working activities (Bergin and Lambert, 1978; Garfield and Bergin, 1971a, 1971b, 1973, 1978; Gazda, 1971, 1972, 1973a, 1973b; Gladstern, 1977; Gomes-Schwartz, Hadley and Strupp, 1978; Gurman, 1977; Hurst and Hefele, 1973; Ivey, 1972, 1973; Kagan, 1972; Korn and Korn, 1972; Lambert, 1983; Lambert and DeJulio, 1977; Lambert, DeJulio and Stern, 1978; Marshall and Kurtz, 1982; Matarazzo, 1978; Mitchell, Bozarth and Krauft, 1977; Morris and Sucherman, 1974a, 1974b, 1975; Mosher and Sprinthall, 1971; Parloff, Waskow and Wolfe, 1978; Resnikoff, 1972, 1973; Sprinthall, 1972; Sprinthall and Erickson, 1973; Truax and Mitchell, 1971).

The confusion is in part a result of the disregard of both systematic intervention designs and their effects. In this context, it may be a function of the inability of many professionals to see HRD in the larger perspective of human productivity. The issues of human productivity revolve around whether the HRD activities make a difference in the real-life functioning of the recipients (Can they meet the requirements of their real-life contexts?) and the costs and benefits to the organizational or societal system in which they function (How can we minimize resource inputs and maximize results outputs?) (Anthony, 1979; Anthony, Buell, Sharratt and Althoff, 1972; Anthony and Drasgow, 1978; Aspy, 1972a, 1973; Aspy, Aspy and Roebuck, 1982; Banks and Anthony, 1973; Barrett-Lennard, 1971; Bellingham, 1978a; Carkhuff, 1972a, 1972b, 1972c, 1982a, 1982b, 1983b).

This confusion has culminated in challenges to the promulgators of HRD programs to this effect: the promulgators must demonstrate the lasting effects of their HRD programs on observable and measurable outcomes illustrating recipient benefits. Specifically, the challenges relate to the effects of helper interpersonal skills (IPS) on recipient living, learning, and working outcome indices. The purpose of this article is to address these challenges by presenting the evidence of outcome studies conducted over the past 15 years.

In this context, Carkhuff (1983b) has defined five levels of intervention outcomes: 1) the interaction between helpers and recipients wherein the helpers facilitate the recipients' involvement in a learning or re-learning experience (process); 2) the recipients' demonstration of the new responses (acquisition); 3) the recipients' demonstration of the responses in simulated real-life experiences (application); 4) the recipients' demonstration of the responses in real-life experiences (transfer); and 5) the recipients' benefits as well as the concomitant costs based on the demonstration of the responses (productivity). In the current article, we have attempted to emphasize outcomes from levels 4 (transfer) and 5 (productivity).

These outcome discriminations mean that many studies of counseling and teaching and working process interactions are omitted. This includes a wealth of revealing process interactions and manipulation studies (reviewed in Berenson and Carkhuff, 1967; Berenson and Mitchell, 1974; Carkhuff, 1969; Carkhuff and Berenson, 1967; Truax and Carkhuff, 1967). For example, the following studies are excluded: the effects of helper IPS upon recipient problem exploration (Berenson and Mitchell, 1974; Cannon and Pierce, 1968; Holder, Carkhuff and Berenson, 1967; Truax and Carkhuff, 1967) the effects of recipient exploration upon helper level of functioning (Alexik and Carkhuff, 1967; Carkhuff and Alexik, 1967; Friel, Kratochvil and Carkhuff, 1968); the effects of helper IPS upon recipient test performance (Holder, Drasgow and Pierce, 1970); accuracy of helper perceptions of recipients (Genther and Sacuzzo, 1977); recipient medical information (Blalock and Aspy, 1979); recipient verbal conditioning (Vitalo, 1970); recipient career-information seeking behavior (Mickelson and Stevic, 1971); and recipient suggestibility (Murphy and Rowe, 1977).

In addition, studies measuring the acquisition of new responses are excluded. A number of studies employed a variety of treatment or training control conditions to establish the efficacy of systematic IPS training. Systematic IPS training emphasized the programmatic teaching, modeling, and shaping of behavior in an experientially consistent context. These studies tend to relte helper level of IPS to recipient level of interpersonal processing (Carkhuff, Kratochvil and Friel, 1968; Pierce, Schauble and Wilson, 1971). They also tend to converge the perceptions of helpers and recipients upon IPS. Other works review these acquisition studies further for helpers (Carkhuff, 1969; Truax and Carkhuff, 1967), teachers (Aspy and Roebuck, 1976, 1977) and employers (Holder, 1982).

Finally, studies assessing the application of new responses in the treatment or training context are omitted. A number of studies employ simulated behavioral rehearsals in the training context as successive approximations of outcome. For example, within the context of treating or training, recipients may attempt to deal with "significant others" who present the same difficult problems that led to the helping or training experience (Carkhuff and Banks, 1970). Other works review these treatment or training application outcomes in helping (Anthony, 1979; Carkhuff, 1971b; Carkhuff and Berenson, 1976), teaching (Aspy and Roebuck, 1976, 1977) and working experiences (Holder, 1982).

5 Mega-Research Design

The outcome studies presented here follow a mega-research design. Basically, that design involves summarizing the findings from all studies of interpersonal productivity. The intervention designs range from simple applications to complex, replicated Latin Square designs. The statistical analyses range from simple frequency tabulations or non-parametric analyses to complex response-surface analyses. The power in the mega-research comes from the variability of the intervention designs and analyses. If the trends are so powerful that they emerge under a variety of conditions, then they are statistically significant trends with significant human implications. Conversely, if the trends are so fragile that they emerge only under carefully controlled circumstances, then they are statistically significant trends with insignificant human implications or meaning.

The outcome studies, then, include large-scale demonstrations as well as experimental studies. They are organized in a 2 x 3 matrix (see Table 1). The component areas of the matrix are two-fold: 1) the effects of interveners or helpers upon recipient outcome indices; and 2) the effects of the direct training of recipients upon recipient outcome indices. The three functional outcome levels include the following: 1) living outcomes, 2) learning outcomes, and 3) working outcomes.

As can be seen, Table 2 (Living Outcomes) involves 22 studies of 25,682 helpees. Tables 3 and 4 (Learning Outcomes) involve 32 studies of 81, 298 learners. Table 5 (Working Outcomes) involves 22 studies of 33,836 employees or prospective employees.

In turn, Table 6 (Living Outcomes) involves 35 studies of 2,279 helpees. Table 7 (Learning Outcomes) involves 26 studies of 3,610 learners. Table 8 (Working Outcomes) involves 27 studies of 12,177 employees.

The studies of the effects of interveners upon recipients total 76 studies of 140,816 recipients. The studies of the direct training of recipients total 88 studies of 18,066 recipients. The grand total is 164 studies of 158,882 recipients.

Table 1. An Index of Tables for the Studies of Living, Learning, and Working Outcomes

SOURCES OF EFFECT

OUTCOMES	INTERVENERS (Indirect effects of helpers upon recipients)	RECIPIENTS (Direct effects of training helpees)
LIVING	Table 2 (22 studies) 25,682 Helpees	Table 6 (35 studies) 2,279 Helpees
LEARNING	Tables 3 and 4 (32 studies) 81,298 Learners	Table 7 (26 studies) 3,610 Learners
WORKING	Table 5 (22 studies) 33,836 Employees	Table 8 (27 studies) 12,235 Employees
Subtotal	(76 studies) 140,816 Recipients	(88 studies) 18,124 Recipients
Grand Total	(164 studies) 158,940 Recipients	

The studies of the effects of interveners upon recipients total 76 studies of 140,816 recipients. The studies of the direct training of recipients total 88 studies of 18,066 recipients. The grand total is 164 studies of 158,882 recipients.

The process by which these functional outcomes are achieved in the component areas will be described in the study, method, and results sections within each component area and functional level. The studies are presented by their nature, author(s), and the date of publication. The methods include the number (N) of the population, the outcome measures, and the time the measures were taken. The results involve those for the treatment condition and the control condition.

The control condition may involve treatment control groups and time control groups. In some instances, the recipient populations provide their own controls as when pre-intervention data are compared with post-intervention data. In some instances, base-rate data from relevant populations is employed as a basis for comparison. The differences are presented according to whether they are significant ($p \leq .05$) and positive (*), non-significant (N.S.), significant, and negative (Neg.) or not applicable (N/A). In some cases, in the interest of communication, indices are collapsed for the presentation.

The matrix is elaborated in Tables 2–8. Table 2 describes the studies of helper effects upon helpee living outcome indices. Tables 3 and 4 describe the research concerning the effects of teachers or teacher-helpers on student or learner learning outcome indices. Because of the extraordinary effort involves, Table 4 is added to highlight a section of extensive and monumental studies by Aspy, Roebuck and their associates in the National Consortium for Humanizing Education. Table 5 describes the effects of employers or employment-helpers on employees or prospective employees.

In turn, Table 6 details the effects of the direct training of general helpee populations. Table 7 describes the direct training of learners. Finally, Table 8 elaborates the direct training of employees.

The measures emphasize indices of real-life behavior (Level 4 of outcome) and estimates of the productivity of that behavior (Level 5 of outcome). The time the measurements are taken ranges from immediately to 13 years following the intervention. Where available, the data are presented for the reader's review. The statements of significance reflect either the researchers' reports or a recalculation based on the collapsing of results. In the absence of comparative data, some of the significance tests of the data are not applicable (N/A).

It is important to emphasize that there were 81 different primary sources for the 166 studies, as indicated by primary authorship. Only two authors, Aspy (11) and Carkhuff (14), were listed as primary authors more than ten times while one author, Vitalo, was listed eight times. Several more researchers had more than two citations while most authors were listed as primary sources one or two times.

6 **The Effects of Interveners on Recipients**

The effects of interveners upon recipients involve the study of people assuming the intervention or helping role upon people in the recipient role. Interveners include people such as parents, counselors, therapists, teachers, and employers. Recipients include people such as children, counselees, patients, learners, and employees. Under living outcomes, we find the effects of both credentialed and lay helpers on helpees' life functioning and productivity. Under learning outcomes, we see the effects of teacher and teacher-helpers on students' learning functioning and productivity. Finally, under working outcomes, we see the effects of employers and employer-helpers upon employees' working functioning and productivity.

Living Outcomes

The living outcomes depicting the effects of helpers upon recipient functionality may be found in Table 2. The 22 living outcome studies emphasize child, youth, and adult behavior and benefits. The *N*'s of the helpee populations range from 8 to 9,877 with a total of 25,682 helpees. The *N*'s of the helper populations range from two to 11,005 with a total of 11,552 helpers. The measures emphasize behavioral observations and recidivism and relapse data. The time at which the measurements were taken ranges from six weeks to six years following the initial treatment intervention.

Table 2. Effects of Helpers Upon Helpees

STUDY				METHOD		RESULTS			
Nature	Authors	Dates	N of Population	Measures	Time	Treatment	Control	Diff.	
1) Child Behavior	Bendix	1977	72 Children (72 Parents)	Behavior Problems Self-Concept				* N.S.	
2) Child Behavior	Bushee & Chapados	1978	37 Children (23 Parents)	Behavior Problems	1 year	3.5/mo.	17/mo.	*	
3) Youth Adjustment	Carkhuff, Devine, et al	1974	321 Youth 1,345 TAP (80 Staff)	Recidivism Community Crime	1 year "	16% (-34%) -34%	24%	*	
4) Youth Adjustment	Scott, Warner, et al	1982	3,896 Youth (12 Staff)	Recidivism	6 yrs.	20.10 – 21%	60 – 62.80%	*	
5) Youth Adjustment	Wiggins	1978	30 Counselees (30 Counselors)	Behavior Indices	6 wks.	39.67	38.47	*	
6) Youth Adjustment	Bopp, Bushee, et al	1978b	1,950 Youth (123 Staff)	Successful Action Client Satisfaction	3 mos. "	92% 99%		N/A N/A	
7) Youth Adjustment	Maloney & Chapados	1978	206 Youth (6 Staff)	Successful Crisis Mediation	14 mos	90%	11.50%	*	

Table 2 (Continued)

Nature	Authors	Dates	N of Population	Measures	Time	Treatment	Control	Diff.
						RESULTS		
	STUDY			**METHOD**				
8) Youth Adjustment	Bouie & Chapados	1978	60 Counselees (60 Counselors)	Client Satisfaction	10 mos	96%	44%	*
				Career Goals	"	91%	25%	*
				Career Courses	"	87%	31%	*
9) Youth Adjustment	Bellingham & Devine	1978	252 Pregnant Girls (7 Child Care Workers)	*Reduced*				
				Lockouts	1 day	1–3	10	*
				Home referrals	2 wks	1	5	*
				Expulsions	"	0	2	*
				Office referrals	"	6–8	9	*
				Hostile expression	"	4–6	10	*
				Incomplete units	"	40	40	N.S.
				Negative—verbal	"	20–30%	40%	*
				Negative—Nonverbal	"	20–30%	40%	*
				Distracting behavior	"	10%	20–25%	*
				Grooming (poor)	"	5%	5–9%	*
				Hygiene (poor)	"	10%	10–19%	*
				Posture (poor)	"	10%	20–25%	*
				Clothing (poor)	"	5%	10–15%	*
				Vandalism	"	5%	8	*
				Present (poor)	"	10%	10–19%	*

Table 2 (Continued)

STUDY			METHOD			RESULTS		
Nature	Authors	Dates	N of Population	Measures	Time	Treatment	Control	Diff.
9) Youth Adjustment (continued)	Bellingham & Devine	1978		Venereal disease	1 mo.	4	3%	Neg.
				Child neglect	"	2	2	N.S.
				Child abuse	"	2	2	N.S.
				Fights	6 mos.	1	2	*
				Weapons	"	0	2	*
				Pregnancies	"	6–7	8	*
				Improved				
				Kind behavior	2 wks.	40–59%	40%	*
				Polite behavior	"	40–59%	40–59%	N.S.
				Decent behavior	"	61–80%	20%	*
				Participatory behavior	"			
				Constructive questions	"	15%	15%	N.S.
				Contributory behavior	"	10–19%	20–24%	Neg.
				Initiative behavior	"	5%	10–20%	*
				Responsive behavior	"	20%	20–39%	Neg.
				Discipline	2 wks.	76–90%	25–49%	*
				Positive behavior	"	76–90%	25%	*
						40–60%	20–39%	*

Table 2 (Continued)

The Effects of Interveners on Recipients

STUDY			METHOD			RESULTS		
Nature	Authors	Dates	N of Population	Measures	Time	Treatment	Control	Diff.
9) Youth Adjustment (continued)	Bellingham & Devine	1978		Friendly behavior	"	10–19%	10%	*
				Hope expression	"	21–33%	10–20%	*
				Energy	"	10–20%	10–20%	N.S.
				Empathy	"	31–40%	10%	*
				Effectiveness	"	81–90%	40%	*
10) Youth Adjustment	Rocha	1982c	9,877 Elementary students (11,005 Parents)	Clinical referrals	1 year			*
				Parent complaints	"			*
				Parent attendance	"			*
				School/community contact	"			*
11) Patient Adjustment	Pierce, Carkhuff & Berenson	1967	17 Lay Volunteers (2 Counselors)	Completion	Immed.	8 of 8	4 of 9	*
				IPS	"	2.39	1.96	*
				Client Exploration	"	2.80	2.51	*
12) Patient Adjustment	Martin & Carkhuff	1968	24 Graduate Students (2 Counselors)	IPS	Immed			5*
				Counselor ratings	"			*
				Questionnaire charge	"			3*2N.S.
				Client perceptions	"			4*1N.S.
				Other perceptions	".			3*2N.S.

25

Table 2 (Continued)

| STUDY | | | | METHOD | | | RESULTS | | |
Nature	Authors	Dates	N of Population	Measures	Time	Treatment	Control	Diff.
13) Patient Adjustment	Kratochvil, Aspy & Carkhuff	1967	24 Col. Counselees (4 Counselors)	Client exploration Client termination	Immed. "			* *
14) Patient Adjustment	Valle	1981	244 Alcoholics (* Counselors)	Relapse Multi-relapse	2 yrs. "	18% 3%	24–36% 9–17%	* *
15) Patient Adjustment	Drasgow	1981	20 Alcoholics (2 Counselors)	Relapse Multi-relapse Employment	5 yrs. " "	0 0 100%	100% 100% 0	* * *
16) Patient Adjustment	Chapados	1979a	2,275 Patients (23 Staff)	Violent incidents per week per 5 people	6 mos.	1	17.5%	*
17) Patient Adjustment	Carkhuff & Truax	1965a	144 Patients (5 Counselors)	Disturbance improve. Interpersonal improvement Intrapersonal improvement Overall improvement Discharge improve.	3 mos. " " " "	38% 45% 38% 51% 15%	16% 32% 30% 27% 9%	* * * * N.S.

Table 2 (Continued)

	STUDY		METHOD			RESULTS		
Nature	Authors	Dates	N of Population	Measures	Time	Treatment	Control	Diff.
13) Patient Adjustment	Kratochvil, Aspy & Carkhuff	1967	24 Col. Counselees (4 Counselors)	Client exploration Client termination	Immed. "			* *
14) Patient Adjustment	Valle	1981	244 Alcoholics (* Counselors)	Relapse Multi-relapse	2 yrs. "	18% 3%	24–36% 9–17%	* *
15) Patient Adjustment	Drasgow	1981	20 Alcoholics (2 Counselors)	Relapse Multi-relapse Employment	5 yrs. " "	0 0 100%	100% 100% 0	* * *
16) Patient Adjustment	Chapados	1979a	2,275 Patients (23 Staff)	Violent incidents per week per 5 people	6 mos.	1	17.5%	*
17) Patient Adjustment	Carkhuff & Truax	1965a	144 Patients (5 Counselors)	Disturbance improve. Interpersonal improvement Intrapersonal improvement Overall improvement Discharge improve.	3 mos. " " " "	38% 45% 38% 51% 15%	16% 32% 30% 27% 9%	* * * * N.S.

Table 2 (Continued)

	STUDY			METHOD			RESULTS		
Nature	Authors	Dates	N of Population	Measures	Time	Treatment	Control	Diff.	
18) Patient Adjustment	Pagell, Carkhuff & Berenson	1967	8 Patients (8 Counselors)	**Behavior Ratings** Interpersonal func.				*	
				Disturbance				N.S.	
				Self-care				*	
				Socialization				*	
				Improvement				*	
				Expert	6 mos.	88%	16%	*	
				Therapist	"	88%	29%	*	
				Interviewee	"	56%	27%	*	
				Self	"	88%	46%	*	
				Interpersonal Skills					
				Expert	6 mos.	100%	10%	*	
				Therapist	"	100%	30%	*	
				Interviewee	"	80%	43%	*	
				Self	"	80%	47%	*	
				Tape	"	30%	13%	*	
19 Patient Adjustment	Farkas	1980	350 Patients (37 Staff)	Staff IPS	6 mos.			*	
				Patient maladaptive behavior	"			N.S.	
				Patient social behav.	"			N.S.	

28

Table 2 (Concluded)

| STUDY | | | | METHOD | | RESULTS | | |
Nature	Authors	Dates	N of Population	Measures	Time	Treatment	Control	Diff.
20) Patient Adjustment	Jung, Cotton, et al	1976	730 Patients (14 Trainers, 300 Staff)	Census	1 year	614	730	*
				Admission	"	360	456	*
				Re-admission	"	296	311	N.S.
				Discharge	"	254	402	*
21) Patient Adjustment	Roebuck & Hussein	1981	124 F. Patients (8 Physicians)	Duration of interviews	6 mos.	10.10–15.30	8.50–96.00	*
				% successful clinical history	"	75.00–83.40%	40.00–53.10%	*
22) Patient Adjustment	Vitalo	1978	5,021 Patients (21 Staff)	Staff empathy	1 year	2.38–2.75	1.75–2.29	*
				Patient improvement	"	92.00–99.00%	70.00–74.00%	*
						79.00%	49.00–64.00%	*
				Patient skills gain	"	57.00–76.00%	18.00–27.00%	*
				Patient identification skills	"			
				EHS	"	2.97–3.61%	1.70–2.34%	*
				% patient cancellation	"	9.62–10.88%	15.70–19.92%	*

29

In studies of child behavior problems, the children of parents trained in IPS significantly reduced the incidence of behavior problems (Bendix, 1977; Bushee and Chapados, 1978). Interestingly, in the Bendix study, the children trained by parents who were trained as IPS trainers evidenced a significant increase in their written IPS and behavioral attending skills. However, on problem behaviors, while significantly improved over the controls, they were not significantly different from the children of parents who were trained as helpers. Neither group was significantly better than the controls on the children's self-concept. The author offered the explanation that, "the limitations of time had not enabled the trainer group to acquire a sufficient skill level to perform their training tasks adequately, hence, minimizing the distinction between groups". The most critical finding is that the systematic IPS training worked for both parents as helpers and parents as trainers in significantly reducing the child behavior problems it was intended to reduce. The IPS training simply was not directed toward the children's self-concepts.

Studies of youth development and adjustment yield similar results. A project assessing the effects of institutional staff trained in IPS upon recidivism and crime in the community from which the delinquent youth were drawn yielded the following results: recidivism, 34%; crime in the community, 34% (Carkhuff, Devine, Berenson, Griffin, et al., 1974). A youth diversion project training both staff and officers in IPS found the following: the recidivism rate of the 3,896 youth involved over a six-year period stabilized at just over 20%. This compared favorably to the base rate of the control group which stabilized at slightly over 50% (Scott, Warner, Powell and Collingwood, 1982). In both of these studies, the IPS staff training produced precisely what it was intended to do—the reduction of recidivism.

In studies of youth adjustment, Wiggins (1978) found that student counselees demonstrated positive behavioral functioning according to the level of functioning of their counselors. In further studies of youth adjustment, it was found that personnel trained in IPS had a constructive effect upon helpee living outcome indices. Thus, of 1,950 youth calls to a crisis intervention center, 92% successfully developed courses of action (Bopp, Bushee and Chapados, 1978a). Similarly, 90% of youth drug and alcohol crises were successfully mediated by IPS-trained staff (Maloney and Chapados, 1978a).

In turn, IPS training equipped staff to significantly increase not only client satisfaction but also the successful development of career goals and courses of action of minority youth (Bouie and Chapados, 1978). In addition, IPS-trained childcare workers reduced the dysfunctionality and improved the functionality on a number of indices (Bellingham and Devine, 1978). Finally, IPS training for parents reduced child clinical referrals and parent complaints while improving parent attendance and school-community contacts (Rocha, 1982a).

Studies of patient adjustment revealed the differential effects of helper IPS on the following helpee indices: termination (Kratochvil, Aspy and Carkhuff, 1967; Pierce, Carkhuff and Berenson, 1967); helpee IPS (Pierce, Carkhuff and Berenson, 1967; Martin and Carkhuff, 1968) and helpee changes as measured by indices of constructive change, questionnaire, client perceptions, and the perceptions of significant others (Martin and Carkhuff, 1968). All of these studies involved IPS training. The Kratochvil study established the effects of the growth or direction of change in helper levels of functioning upon helpee change or gain.

In studies of adult behavior, reduction in alcoholic relapse (Drasgow, 1981; Valle, 1981) and violent behavior (Chapados, 1979a) were found to be related to helper level of IPS. Drasgow also found that employment and relapse were inversely related over a period of five years; persons who have alcoholic relapses tend to be unemployed over an extended period of time. In his report, Drasgow emphasized that, given the facilitative therapeutic experience provided by the helper to the recipient, a systematic and caring, monitoring follow-up is critical to lasting constructive change. In this context, the continuing vocational, educational, and marital growth of patients over five years was found in other studies by Drasgow and his associates to be related to the active, positive disposition of counselors who offered high levels of IPS (Palau, Leitner, Drasgow, and Drasgow, 1975).

In terms of patient adjustment, Carkhuff and Truax (1965a, 1965b) found significant increases in the ward behavior ratings of the disturbance, interpersonal, intrapersonal, and overall improvement of backward schizophrenic patients treated by IPS-trained ward attendants. In general, 51% of the treated group members improved with only 1% deteriorating while 27% of the control group improved with 17% deteriorating. However, while 11 of 74 (15%) of the treatment patients and only 6 of 70 (9%) of the control patients were discharged as consequences of "blind" staff judgments, the differences were not significant at the .05 level. Again, the help-ing was oriented toward patient institutional adjustment rather than external adjustment, and that is exactly what was achieved. Fur-thermore, it is noteworthy that as the first systematic lay training program in the history of helping, this study was conducted in a hos-tile professional environment.

In a study of external patient adjustment, significant differences in indices of interpersonal functioning, self-care, sociability, and improvement (but not degree of disturbances per se) were found for outpatients of high-functioning IPS counselors as opposed to those of low IPS counselors (Pagell, Carkhuff and Berenson, 1967). Expert, therapist, standard-interviewee, and self-ratings all indicated signifi-cant improvement for the patients of high IPS counselors as did the tape ratings of interpersonal functioning. Patient self-ratings were the least significant discriminators of improvement.

Farkas (1980) was able to demonstrate improvement in staff IPS functioning due to training, but she was unable to relate this improvement to indices of patient maladaptive behavior and social participation. The investigator attributed the lack of results to the lack of support in an essentially hostile institutional setting: "Politics and problems appear to be the greatest deterrents to improving insti-tutional practices." On the other hand, in a supportive institutional environment, it was found that the following patient indices could be changed significantly by training the staff in IPS: patient census total, admissions, recidivism, and discharged (Jung, Cotton, Hume and Emergy, 1976).

In turn, Roebuck and Vitalo and their respective associates were able to demonstrate significant IPS training relationships. Roebuck and Hussein (1981, in Aspy, Aspy and Roebuck, 1982) showed that IPS-trained physicians in two clinics in a Third World country conducted significantly more attentive (duration in minutes) and successful clinical history-taking interviews for infertile women. Vitalo (1978) found that patient improvement, skills gains, and patient identification of gains were improved significantly with the introduction of systematic IPS training. Vitalo emphasizes that the systematic training approach helps to organize the entire treatment effort. Further, in the context of a facilitative therapeutic atmosphere, he emphasizes the level of therapist effort within and following treatment as a critically significant source of effect.

In summary, the effects of helper IPS functioning on helpee living outcomes are demonstrated. Twenty of the 22 studies (91%) had exclusively or predominantly positive results. Ninety-four of 114 indices (83%) yielded positive results. It is noteworthy that in all instances, systematic IPS training was the source of helper functionality and, thus, recipient outcomes. Even in the Wiggins and Valle studies where the helpers were not trained to achieve the outcomes in the reported studies, they were trained in IPS in previous demonstrations not directly related to the reported studies. Further, it is important to recognize the emphasis upon follow-up efforts as a significant source of constructive recipient benefits. Finally, the issue of environmental support looms large in facilitating or retarding the gains of training, treatment, and follow-up.

Learning Outcomes

The 32 learning outcome studies representative of the effects of teachers or teacher-helpers on student learning outcomes may be found in Tables 3 and 4. In Table 3, the 22 learning outcome studies emphasize student discipline, learner involvement, and learner achievement. The *N*'s of the learner populations range from 14 students to 49,885 students with a total of 61, 907 students involved. The *N*'s of the teacher-helper populations range from 6 to 1,987 with a total of 2,437 teachers and helpers involved. The measures emphasize student discipline and learner involvement and achievement measures. The time at which the measurements were taken ranges from immediately to a study of the cumulative effects of intervention over a nine-year period.

In studies of student discipline, Banks and his associates (1981) found the teachers' levels of IPS to be related inversely to the use of the paddle for discipline problems, vandalism, bus incidents, discipline referrals, fights, and the time needed to teach a lesson. In similar efforts with secondary students, Unger and others (1979a, 1979b) found teacher IPS to be positively related to positive student attitude and negatively related to student lack of preparation, tardiness, disruption, absenteeism, and arrests.

Other studies produced consistent related results. Teacher IPS was found to be related negatively to the time needed to start teaching, disciplinary referrals, and classroom disruptions and positively related to secondary student task performance, catching problems in student assignments, and classroom participation

Table 3. Effects of Teachers Upon Learners

STUDY			METHOD			RESULTS		
Nature	Authors	Dates	N of Population	Measures	Time	Treatment	Control	Diff.
1) Student Discipline	Banks, Benividez & Bergeson	1981	110 Elementary students (15 Teachers)	Paddle use	1 year	0%	4	*
				Vandalism	"	−50%		*
				Bus incidents	"	3	12	*
				Discipline referrals	"	−90%		*
				Fights	"	−95%		*
				Time to teach	"	−15%		*
2) Student Discipline	Unger, Douds & Pierce	1979a	1,300 Secondary students (40 Teachers)	Positive attitude	1 year	55%	42%	*
				Lack of preparation	"	−83%		*
				Tardiness	"	−80%		*
				Disruptions	"	−67%		*
				Absenteeism	"	−11%	+1%	*
				Arrests	"	−19.5%	+129.5%	*
3) Student Discipline	Benividez, Banks & Bergeson	1981	775 Secondary students (15 Teachers)	Time to start	1 year	−100%		*
				Discipline referrals	"	−67%		*
				Class disruption	"	−75%		*
				Student tasks	"	+28%		*
				Student assignment	"	+88%		*
				Class participation	"	+53%		*

Table 3. (Continued)

STUDY				METHOD		RESULTS		
Nature	Authors	Dates	N of Population	Measures	Time	Treatment	Control	Diff.
4) Student Discipline	Berenson & Savidge	1981	300 Secondary students (30 Teachers)	Discipline referrals Suspensions	1 year "	−55% −33%		* *
5) Student Discipline	Geary & Chapados	1980	2,240 Secondary students (14 Teachers)	Problems class/day Drug arrests student/year	1 year "	.9 1/17	3 1/22	* *
6) Student Discipline	Gorbette & Chapados	1980	1,200 College students (6 Counselors)	Unresolved problems Counselor referrals Discipline problems Student complaints	5 mos. " " "	8 11 31 5	72 43 122 24	* * * *
7) Learner Involvement	Stoffer	1970	35 Elementary students (35 Helpers)	*Combined Change Index* Intelligence Achievement Behavior Motivation				

Table 3. (Continued)

Nature	STUDY Authors	Dates	N of Population	METHOD Measures	Time	RESULTS Treatment	Control	Diff.
7) Learner Involvement (continued)				Correlated with: Warmth Empathy Student relations Helper relations	3 mos. " " "	.40 .32 .41 .29		* * * N.S.
8) Learner Involvement	Greenberg & Vitalo	1981	330 Elementary students (11 Teachers)	Detractive rating Contributory rating	1 mo. "	21% 71%	35% 65%	* *
9) Learner Involvement	Carkhuff & Friel	1974	75 Secondary students (25 Teachers/Counselors)	Career impact Career plans Career preparation Counselor impact	Immed. " " "	74—91% 87—100% —60% 67—100%	13—67% 78—91% 58—85% 21—91%	* N.S. N.S. *
10) Learner Involvement	Berenson	1971	1,500 Secondary students (25 Teachers/Counselors)	Pupil initiative	2 mos.	6.70	4—6.40	*

Table 3. (Continued)

The Effects of Interveners on Recipients

STUDY				METHOD		RESULTS		
Nature	Authors	Dates	N of Population	Measures	Time	Treatment	Control	Diff.
11) Learner Involvement	Davison	1976c	14 Students (14 Tutors)	Self-esteem	3 mos.	348.36	342.86	N.S.
				Self-realization needs	"	99.29	95.57	*
				Transcendence	"	107.71	107.36	N.S.
				Social needs	"	2.59	2.14	*
				Respect from others	"	4.06	3.83	*
				Dogmatism	"	−48.00	−38.70	N.S.
				Belonging	"	1.10	1.00	N.S.
				Self-esteem	"	343.62	337.31	N.S.
				Self-realization needs	"	92.00	86.94	N.S.
				Transcendence	"	106.22	104.33	N.S.
				Social needs	"	2.23	1.77	*
				Respect from others	"	3.89	3.50	*
				Self-reality processing	"	4.32	2.65	*
12) Learner Involvement	Leonidas	1976b	24 Vulnerable elementary students (24 Community volunteers)	General anxiety	3 mos.	16.95	19.50	N.S.
				Self-anxiety	"	6.17	6.42	*
				Popularity	"	7.71	6.21	*
				Behavior	"	13.08	11.17	*
				Intellectual	"	12.96	11.79	*
				Physical	"	8.00	6.71	*
				Happiness	"	6.83	5.96	*

Table 3. (Continued)

STUDY				METHOD		RESULTS		
Nature	Authors	Dates	N of Population	Measures	Time	Treatment	Control	Diff.
12) Learner Involvement (Continued)				Overall	"	53.75	47.21	*
				Feeling	"	33.54	29.75	*
				Thinking	"	13.75	13.38	N.S.
				Overall	"	19.79	16.38	*
13) Learner Involvement	Bellingham	1978a	500 Elementary students (20 Teachers)	**Teacher Evaluation (by Teachers)**				
				Teacher effectiveness	1 year	3.0	2.3	*
				Student choices	"	3.0	1.9	*
				Paraphrasing	"	2.7	1.8	*
				Responding	"	3.1	2.2	*
				Identifying reasons	"	3.0	2.1	*
				Student self-expression	"	3.2	2.4	*
				Repeat content	"	2.2	1.8	*
				Face student	"	3.2	2.8	*
				Noting student relations	"	2.7	2.0	*
				Goal-setting	"	2.7	1.8	*
				Focusing on student	"	3.1	2.3	*
				Reflecting mood	"	2.9	2.2	*
				Emphasize student values	"	2.5	1.9	*

The Effects of Interveners on Recipients

Table 3. (Continued)

| STUDY | | | METHOD | | | RESULTS | | |
Nature	Authors	Dates	N of Population	Measures	Time	Treatment	Control	Diff.
13) Learner Involvement (Continued)				Identify concrete goals	"	2.6	2.0	*
				Facilitate student exploration	"	2.8	2.0	*
				Suspend judgment	"	3.0	2.3	*
				Close distance	"	3.2	2.5	*
				Noting student feelings	"	3.5	2.9	*
				Noting immediacy		3.0	2.3	*
				Respond to meaning	"	2.7	2.2	*
				Respond physically	"	3.0	2.4	*
				Noting student energy	"	3.1	2.5	*
				Facilitate exploring content	"	2.7	2.2	
				Resisting distractions	"	3.0	2.6	*
				Noting student behavior	"	3.4	3.0	*
				Eliminate distractions	"	3.1	2.8	*
				Noting student values	"	2.9	2.9	*
				Eye contact	"	3.3	3.0	*
				Noting student appearance	"	3.0	2.6	*

Table 3. (Continued)

| STUDY | | | METHOD | | | RESULTS | | |
Nature	Authors	Dates	N of Population	Measures	Time	Treatment	Control	Diff.
13) Learner Involvement (Continued)				***Student Evaluation (by Teachers)***				
				Personal readiness	1 year	3.2	2.0	*
				Identifying feelings	"	3.0	1.8	*
				Awareness of feelings	"	3.1	2.0	*
				Aware of choices	"	3.0	1.7	*
				Receive directions	"	2.9	1.9	*
				Material readiness	"	3.0	1.9	*
				Viewing teacher	"	3.3	2.0	*
				Leaning toward teacher	"	2.5	1.5	*
				Holding still	"	2.7	1.6	*
				Presentation proud	"	2.9	2.0	*
				Organize materials	"	2.7	1.7	*
				Organize directions	"	2.8	1.7	*
				Recall facts	"	3.0	1.9	*
				Check assignment	"	2.9	1.9	*
				Choose positive response	"	3.0	1.9	*
				Consider others' feelings	"	2.9	2.0	*
				Identify choices	"	2.4	1.6	*

Table 3. (Continued)

STUDY			METHOD			RESULTS		
Nature	Authors	Dates	N of Population	Measures	Time	Treatment	Control	Diff.
13) Learner Involvement (Concluded)				Org. reading material	"	2.9	2.0	*
				Clear head	"	2.6	1.8	*
				Identify consequences	"	2.9	2.0	*
				Be polite	"	2.9	2.2	*
				Be respectful	"	2.9	2.2	*
				Keep desks neat	"	2.2	1.7	*
				Teacher Evaluation (by Students)				
				Teacher effectiveness	"	2.9%	1.8	*
				Student effectiveness	"	76—98%		N/A
				Clear head	"	92%		N/A
				Basic interrogatives	"	84%		N/A
				Check steps	"	71%		N/A
				Ask questions	"	87%		N/A
				Identify feelings	"	76%		N/A
				Identify choices	"	85%		N/A
				Identify implications	"	82%		N/A
				Choose alternative	"	90%		N/A
				Politeness	"	94%		N/A
				Empathy	"	92%		N/A
				Kindness	"	96%		N/A

Table 3. (Continued)

STUDY			METHOD			RESULTS		
Nature	Authors	Dates	N of Population	Measures	Time	Treatment	Control	Diff.
14) Learner Achievement	Kratochvil, Carkhuff & Berenson	1969	350 Elementary students (12 Teachers)	Reading achievement	9 years cum.			N.S.
15) Learner Achievement	Hefele	1971	99 Secondary students (31 Teachers)	Reading achievement Math achievement	5 mos. "	r = .79 r = .43		* *
16) Learner Achievement	Egloff	1972	20 Secondary students (20 Teachers/ Helpers)	Reading achievement	3 mos.	+ 2 years	3 mos.	*
17) Learner Achievement	Mallory & Battenschlag	1979	600 Secondary students (40 Teachers)	Teacher IPS Teacher model development Learner life comprehension Facts and concepts Principles Skills	3 mos. " " " " "			* * * N.S. *

Table 3. (Continued)

The Effects of Interveners on Recipients

STUDY			METHOD			RESULTS		
Nature	Authors	Dates	N of Population	Measures	Time	Treatment	Control	Diff.
18) Learner Achievement	Williams & Barnet	1979	50 College students (2 Teachers)	Educational psychology skills	3 mos.	+ 41%	+ 26%	*
19) Learner Achievement	Kenney	1972	350 Elementary students (18 Teachers)	I.Q.	1 year	+ 15		*
				Reading achievement	"	+ 1.5 Gr.		*
				Parent involvement	"	100%	0	*
				Discipline	"	0	30%	*
				School rank	"	23 of 176	176 of 176	*
20) Learner Achievement	Middlebrooks	1976	350 Elementary students (20 Teachers)	Reading achievement	1 year	+ 7 mos.		*
				Math achievement	"	+ 7 mos.		*
				Pupil absenteeism	"	3.9%	7.1%	*
				Teacher turnover	"	0	80%	*
				Vandalism	"	0	1/wk.	*
				School Rank	"	11.5 of 87	87 of 87	*
21) Learner Achievement	Rochow	1982	1,800 Elementary and secondary students (10 Teachers/ Counselors)	Dropouts	1 year	3%	27%	*
				Attendance	"	+ 66%		*
				Involvement	"	90%	10%	*
				Grade point average	"	3.0	1.5	*
				Parent participation	"	76%	4%	*

Table 3. (Concluded)

STUDY				METHOD		RESULTS		
Nature	Authors	Dates	N of Population	Measures	Time	Treatment	Control	Diff
22) Learner Achievement	Rocha	1982a	49,885 Elementary students (1,987 Teachers, Counselors, Supervisors, Directors, Secretaries, Custodians, Librarians, Food service workers)	Enrollment	2 yrs.	+ 9—15%		*
				Dropouts	"	1.8—3.3%	2.5—5.0%	*
				Attendance	1 year	24.8—35.5%	31.1—48.5%	*
				IPS	"	75% below 3.0 91—95% app.	95% above 3.0	*
				IPS	"	91—94% pos.		N/A
				Self-report	"	76% inc.		N/A
				Cooperation	"	75% inc.		N/A
				Enthusiasm	"	65% dec.		N/A
				Gossip	"	73% inc.		N/A
				Problem solving	"			N/A
				Relationships				
				Teachers	"	79% inc.		N/A
				Special teachers	"	69% inc.		N/A
				Support staff	"	56% inc.		N/A
				Family	"	64% inc.		N/A
				Parents	"	69% inc.		N/A
				Students	"	79% inc.		N/A
				Supervisor evaluation	"	91% pos.		N/A
				Teacher-Student involvement	"	75% imp.		N/A

44

(Benividez, Banks and Bergeson, 1981). These results were replicated for secondary student discipline referrals and suspensions
(Berenson and Savidge, 1981). The IPS outcomes were further
extended to the reduction of classroom problems and drug arrests
(Geary and Chapados, 1980) and the reduction of unresolved problems, counselor referrals, discipline problems, and student complaints to the Dean (Gorbette and Chapados, 1980).

Stoffer's early study (1970) of the effects of teacher-helper IPS
on student behavior changes produced limited results. He found
helper warmth and empathy in the student relationship inventory
(but not the helper relationship inventory) related to a combined
student change index assessing student intelligence, achievement,
classroom behavior, and motivation over a limited time period. What
is noteworthy about this study is that Stoffer got any effects at all
given the restrictiveness of functioning of an untrained helper population. In a later study, Greenberg and Vitalo (1981) found that disruptive behavior was reduced and contributory behavior increased
in classrooms using IPS-trained teachers.

Studies of learner involvement found student-counselee self-
reports in real-life career counseling favoring counselors trained in
IPS and other HRD skills over counselors untrained in HRD skills
(Carkhuff and Friel, 1974). Interestingly, the impact of career counseling on counselees was as follows: "motivated" counselors who
saw counselees for more than the usual five minutes were twice as
effective as "unmotivated" counselors (26% to 13%); the computer-
based career guidance program was twice as effective as motivated
counselors (50% to 26%); the computer-trained counselor in conjunction with the computer-based program was one-third more
effective than the computer alone (67% to 50%); and HRD-trained
counselors, in conjunction with the computer (74%) and independent of the computer (91%), were between 10% and 36% more effective than the computer-trained counselors. In sum, systematic IPS
training improved the impact of counselors from 3.5 to seven times,
depending on whether "motivated" (26% effective) or "unmotivated"
counselors (13% effective) were employed as the base rate.

In further studies of learner involvement, Berenson (1971)
found pupil initiative to be a function of teacher IPS. In a prototypical
research design, four treatment groups were employed: the experimental group, the training-control group, the Hawthorne-effect
group, and the control group proper. Berenson found differences
between the competencies of teachers in the experimental group and

those in all of the control groups. Most important, the pupils in the experimental group spent significantly more time initiating with the teacher and with each other than pupils under other conditions who generally reacted to teacher directions.

Bierman and his associates (1976) conducted a number of studies of learner involvement. They found that tutees changed selectively on self-concept measures while the tutors were also changing (Davison, 1976a). They also found that vulnerable elementary students changed constructively on measures of experience and behavior (Leonidas, 1976a).

Bellingham (1978a) conducted a study of behavioral indices of learner involvement. He found that teachers evaluated teachers' improvement positively on all indices. In turn, teachers rated learners' improvement positively. Finally, students evaluated teachers as having improved significantly in their effectiveness. Without pre-measures for control, 71%–96% of the students also evaluated themselves positively in terms of their involvement behavior.

In studies of learner achievement. Kratochvil and his associates (1969), while relating the effects of outstanding individual teachers to learner achievement, failed to establish the cumulative effects of parent and teacher interpersonal skills upon learner achievement. One of the reasons for this was the random selection of the teacher population. Hefele (1971), in turn, established further individual relationships between trained-teacher IPS and learner achievement in reading and arithmetic. Finally, Egloff (1972) was able to produce two years of reading growth in three months with slow readers by training tutor-helpers to employ IPS programmatically. Again, where IPS training is present, the variability in teaching is increased and the positive effects on learners are demonstrated directly.

In studies of student achievement in life-role competencies, Mallory and Battenschlag (1979) found that training teachers in IPS and module development significantly improved their teaching deliveries. The learners mastered significantly more facts, concepts, skills, and skill steps (but not principles). Similarly, Williams (1979), in Aspy, Aspy and Roebuck (1982), found that students of teachers trained in IPS achieved significantly more in educational psychology skills than students of teachers without such training.

In further studies of learner achievement, both Kenney (in Aspy, 1972b) and Middlebrooks (in Aspy and Roebuck, 1976) trained the entire teaching staffs of schools servicing disadvantaged students. Kenney found significant improvements in intelligence (15 I.Q.

points) and reading (gaining seven months more over the course of the school year than the previous year). He also found significant improvements in student discipline and parental involvement. The school's ranking moved from 176th of 176 schools to 23rd of 176 in one year.

Middlebrooks, in turn, found seven months' improvement in reading and math achievement over previous years. Pupil absenteeism and vandalism was reduced and teacher turnover eliminated. The school's ranking moved from 87th of 87 schools to a tie for 11th of 87 schools. In both cases, Kenney and Middlebrooks directly attributed school improvement to teacher IPS.

Rochow (1982) found that teacher-counselors trained in IPS were able to improve outcome indices of 1,800 elementary and secondary American Latino students. Dropouts decreased from 27% to 3%. Attendance improved 66%. Student involvement in school activities increased from 10% to 90%. Grade point averages (GPAs) improved 100% from 1.5 to 3.0 and parent participation improved extraordinarily from 4% to 76%.

Finally, in one of the largest demonstrations of its kind, Rocha (1982b) implemented a series of studies in a comprehensive school-community design. Training several thousand members of school staff and communities, she studies the effects of IPS on tens of thousands of Brazilian elementary school students. Rocha found that the trained adults were able to increase school enrollment while decreasing dropouts and absenteeism. In addition, she demonstrated improvements in a number of relationship indices. Further, she provided anecdotal evidence for the following: increased school achievement; reductions in clinical referrals; improvement in student culturalization, socialization, talent, and recreation responses; and improvement in food services, especially food quantity and quality as well as student malnourishment diagnosis and treatment.

In Table 4, a selection of 10 of the Aspy-Roebuck studies are summarized. These particular studies emphasize student outcomes of discipline, learner involvement, and learner achievement. The Ns of the learner populations range from 50 to 7,408 students with a total of 19,391 students involved. The Ns of the teacher populations range from 2 to 298 with a total of 783 teachers involved. Typically, the authors first conducted small pilot studies before making large-scale demonstrations. The measures employed emphasized a variety of indices of learner development. The time at which the measurements

Table 4. Effects of Teachers Upon Learners: Aspy and Roebuck

STUDY				METHOD		RESULTS		
Nature	Authors	Dates	N of Population	Measures	Time	Treatment	Control	Diff
1) Student Discipline	Aspy & Hadlock	1967	64 Elementary students (2 Teachers)	Days absent	1 year	5.00	9.00	*
2) Student Discipline	Roebuck, Lemoucelli, et al.	1981	317 Ninth grade students (12 Teachers)	Self-esteem	4.5 mos.	68.80	62.80	*
				Problem Solving		8.64	7.03	*
				Values	9 mos.	11.92	11.38	N.S.
				Days tardy	"	2.88	3.13	N.S.
				# extra activities	"	3.08	1.45	*
				# leadership positions	"	.09	.07	*
				# honorable mentions	"	.93	.47	*
				# disciplinary visits	"	.15	.41	*
				# maladaptive behaviors	"	.85	1.84	*
				Grade point average	"	2.67	2.19	*
3) Learner Involvement	Aspy & Roebuck	1976	2,070 Students (69 Teachers)	Involvement index	1 year	3.40	2.83	*
4) Learner Involvement	Aspy & Roebuck	1977	7,408 Students (298 Teachers)	Student responding	6 mos.	36.2%	30.2%	*
				Student initiative	"	7.9%	4.5%	*
				Student thinking	"	2.4%	.8%	*
				Student confusion	"	7.3%	15.0%	*

48

The Effects of Interveners on Recipients

Table 4. (Continued)

	STUDY			METHOD		RESULTS		
Nature	Authors	Dates	N of Population	Measures	Time	Treatment	Control	Diff
5) Learner Achievement	Aspy	1972b	50 Elementary students (2 Teachers)	I.Q.	1 year	+ 9	0	*
6) Learner Achievement	Aspy	1969	120 Elementary students (6 Teachers)	Paragraph meaning	1 year	.99 Gr.	.66	*
				Language	"	1.47	.70	*
				Word meaning	"	.97	.76	*
				Word Skills	"	1.23	.78	*
				Spelling	"	.94	1.10	N.S.
				Total Achievement	"	5.04	4.02	*
7) Learner Involvement	Aspy & Roebuck	1976 1977	2,401 Students (104 Teachers)	*Student Involvement*		Elem. (Sec.)	Elem. (Sec.)	
				Responses	1 year	31.6 (36.2%)	25.1 (30.2%)	*(*)
				Initiatives	"	6.6 (7.9%)	5.8 (4.5%)	*(*)
				Confusion	"	5.8 (7.3%)	13.9 (15.9%)	*(*)
				Recalls facts	"	32.9 (39.4%)	28.3 (33.7%)	*(*)
				Asks for facts	"	1.8 (2.4%)	1.8 (.6%)	*(*)
				Thinks	"	2.7 (2.4%)	.7 (.8%)	*(*)
				Asks for thinking	"	.2 (1.0%)	.1 (0%)	*(*)
				Non-cognitive behavior	"	1.2 (5.0%)	.8 (2.2%)	*(*)
				Silence or chaos	"	4.6 (8.3%)	12.9 (15.4%)	*(*)

49

Table 4. (Continued)

STUDY			METHOD		RESULTS		
Nature	Authors	Dates	N of Population	Measures	Time	Treatment	Control	Diff

Nature	Authors	Dates	N of Population	Measures	Time	Treatment	Control	Diff
7) Learner Involvement (Continued)				*Reading Achievement*				
				Grades 1–3	1 year	13.66	2.78	*
				Grades 4–6	"	5.83	2.17	*
				Grades 7–9	"	−6.44	−8.40	*
				Grades 10–12	"	2.89	1.33	*
				Math Achievement				
				Grades 4–6	"	10.10	−5.34	*
				Grades 7–9	"	−16.58	−20.64	*
				Grades 10–12	"	3.47	1.53	*
				English Achievement				
				Grades 4–6	"	—	—	*
				Grades 7–9	"	3.47	−8.97	*
				Grades 10–12	"	.50	1.46	N.S.
				Self-Concept				
				Grades 1–3	"	.99	−1.97	*
				Grades 4–6	"	2.66	−.18	*
				Grades 7–9	"	7.61	.83	*
				Grades 10–12	"	1.78	−.31	*

Table 4. (Continued)

Nature	STUDY Authors	Dates	N of Population	METHOD Measures	Time	RESULTS Treatment	Control	Diff
8) Learner Achievement	Aspy & Roebuck	1976 1977	6,412 Students (272 Teachers)	**Days Absent**				
				Grades 1–3	2 yrs.	6.44	8.94	*
				Grades 4–6	"	4.98	8.35	*
				Grades 7–9	"	7.15	10.11	*
				Grades 10–12	"	8.30	12.13	*
				Reading Achievement				
				Grades 1–3	2 yrs.	21.57	17.55	*
				Grades 4–6	"	−2.22	−3.23	N.S.
				Grades 10–12	"	8.92	4.22	*
				Math Achievement				
				Grades 4–6	2 yrs.	1.07	−10.43	*
				Grades 10–12	"	−10.42	−5.04	Neg.
				English Achievement				
				Grades 4–6	2 yrs.	17.80	2.55	*
				Grades 10–12	"	7.31	11.15	*
				Self-Concept				
				Grades 3–6	2 yrs.	8.61	1.08	*
				Grades 7–12	"	6.85	.92	*

Table 4. (Concluded)

STUDY			METHOD				RESULTS		
Nature	Authors	Dates	N of Population	Measures	Time	Treatment	Control	Diff	
9) Learner Behavior	Roebuck	1979	106 Youth (6 Staff)	Knowledge	1 mo.	8.53	5.93	*	
				Focus of control	"	1.65	-.05	*	
				Attitudes to contraception	"	4.28	4.18	N.S.	
10) Learner Behavior	Roebuck	1981	443 Female youth (12 Staff)	% pregnancies	1 year	9.3%	15.2—20.8%	*	
				% contraception	"	75.0%	32.9—71.6%	*	
				% problems	"	18.1%	17.8—35.0%	*	
				% negative	"	16.5%	21.1—26.5%	*	

were taken ranges from two months to two years following the teaching interventions. These outcome studies are drawn from more than 50 studies of teaching and teacher training conducted by Aspy, Roebuck and their associates in most of the United States as well as many countries around the world (Aspy, 1972b; Aspy and Roebuck, 1976, 1977).

In one of the early studies relating teacher IPS to student discipline, Aspy and Hadlock (1967, 1976) found that the students of a teacher offering low levels of IPS were absent significantly more than the students of a matched but untrained teacher offering high levels of IPS. In an expanded demonstration of the effects of IPS training upon discipline, Roebuck and her associates (Roebuck, Lemoucelli, Williams and Memary, 1981, in Aspy, Aspy and Roebuck, 1982) related teacher IPS to a variety of student discipline indices: self-esteem, problem-solving capacity, number of extracurricular activities, leadership positions, number of honorable mentions on report cards, number of disciplinary visits to the principal, total of maladaptive behavior incidents, and GPA. However, the relationships with the study of values and the days of tardiness, while in the predicted direction, were not significant. In general, students of teachers offering high levels of IPS present fewer discipline problems and evidence greater initiative than students of teachers with low levels of IPS.

In studies of learner involvement, Aspy and Roebuck (1976, 1977) found significant relationships between teacher IPS levels and a variety of student involvement measures: involvement, responding, initiative thinking, and student silence or confusion. In general, teachers trained to exhibit high levels of IPS tended to involve students more effectively in the learning process.

It is in studies of learner achievement that Aspy and Roebuck have made their lasting mark. In his classic study of high- and low-IPS functioning teachers, Aspy (1969) found four indices of language meaning (paragraph meaning, language, word meaning, and word skills) to be related to high teacher-IPS functioning and one index of language mechanics (spelling) to be related to low teacher-IPS functioning. Assumedly, the high-functioning teachers concentrated on meaning while the low-functioning teachers emphasized mechanics. In a later study of learner intelligence (I.Q.), Aspy (1972a) found that the students of high-IPS teachers demonstrated a gain of nine I.Q. points while students of low-IPS teachers remained the same over the course of a year. In all of these instances, the teachers involved were carefully selected to insure variability on the IPS index.

In large-scale demonstrations of the effects of teacher training in IPS on rural student achievement, Aspy and Roebuck (1976, 1977) related IPS-trained teachers' levels of functioning to the following learner indices: low absenteeism; high reading achievement (with grades 10–12 the exception); high English achievement; and high self-concepts. In similar large-scale studies of urban student achievement, Aspy and Roebuck (1976, 1977) related trained-teacher IPS skill levels to the following learner indices: reading achievement; math achievement; English achievement (with the exception of grades 10–12); and self-concept development.

In general, the relationship between teacher IPS and absentee-ism and involvement increases slightly with grade level. With grade advancement, students tend to show up more and become more involved with high-IPS teachers. Conversely, teacher IPS appears to have a positive yet declining effect on achievement with increasing grade level. IPS tends to be more influential upon student achieve-ment in the earlier grades. Finally, IPS appears to maintain the potency of its effect across grade levels upon self-concepts (teacher-school, physical appearance, interpersonal, autonomy, and aca-demic), with some distinct tendency for students of untrained teach-ers to make negative changes in aspects of their self-concepts.

Further extensions of this work have been made in the medical arena by Roebuck. First, she established that sexually-active teenag-ers absorbed significantly more knowledge and demonstrated sig-nificantly greater change in locus of control (but not attitudes) in relation to contraception from trained high-IPS teachers than from untrained, low-IPS teachers (Roebuck, 1979, in Aspy, Aspy and Roebuck, 1982). Next, she demonstrated that the students of trained IPS functioning teachers were significantly more positive from the control conditions, including low-IPS teachers, on the following indi-ces: percent of pregnancies incurred during the project year, percent formally developing and committing to a contraception plan, percent sustaining problems with the contraception methods (Roebuck, 1981, in Aspy, Aspy and Roebuck, 1982).

Perhaps the most important summary points that can be made emphasize IPS as the source of effect in learner outcomes: "Appar-ently, entering the students' frames of reference by making inter-changeable responses helps teachers to include the students' goals in their classrooms...A second aspect of the teachers' use of inter-changeable responses...has some support in the teachers' number of a) interchangeable responses and (b) their communication of 'you can do' terms. If the first quality is thought of as empathy and the second as respect, then the data which found a strong positive rela-tionship between them tend to support them as pieces of the same totality (Aspy, 1973)."

In summary, the effects of teacher IPS functioning on student learning outcomes are demonstrated. Twenty-one of the 22 studies (95%) and 132 of the 145 indices (92%) reported in Table 3 yielded positive results. In addition, all ten of the Aspy-Roebuck studies (100%) and 68 of the 74 indices (91%) reported in Table 4 were positive. Overall then, 31 of the 32 studies (97%) and 241 of 261 indices (92%) proved positive.

Again, it is noteworthy that systematically-introduced IPS train-ing is usually involved. Of the 32 studies, 28 involved systematic IPS training. All of the studies that did not involve training were earlier studies that attempted to establish relationships with restricted ranges of IPS functioning. Of these, one yielded non-significant results (Kratochvil, Carkhuff and Berenson, 1969). However, even in the Kratochvil study, the results were meaningful in terms of prac-tice and research. The teacher functioning highest on IPS facilitated learner achievement significantly above all other teachers. Similarly, Aspy's (1969) finding is meaningful in terms of practice and research. The students of high-IPS functioning teachers achieved greater results in areas of meaning while students of low-functioning teachers tended to do as well or better than those of the highs in mechanics, like spelling.

Systematic training is universally the source of teacher IPS. In this context, it is important to emphasize that studies of follow-up programs are omitted from the studies of teaching effectiveness. Furthermore, aside from the studies by Aspy and associates (1976, 1977, 1978) of the effects of principals' levels of IPS on teachers' IPS, there is little attention given to the issue of environmental direction and support of teacher training or teaching gains.

Working Outcomes

The 22 studies of working outcomes reflecting the effects of employ-ers or employer-helpers on employee working outcomes may be found in Table 5. The working outcome studies emphasize worker performance and agency productivity. The N's of the employee populations range from 11 to 15,000 with a total of 33,836 workers. The N's of the employer populations range from 1 to 645 with a total of 1,507 employers or helpers. The measures emphasize various work variables, dollar savings, and other indices of productivity. The time at which the measurements were taken ranges from one month to six years following the intervention.

In studies of worker preparation, IPS-trained employer-counselors were found to have a significant effect on a variety of indices of occupational awareness and decision making as well as the following worker preparation indices: time spent talking to parents, certainty of vocational choice, absenteeism, and vocational maturity. The relationship with grade point average (G.P.A.) did not quite achieve the .05 level of significance (Myers, Thompson, Lindeman, Super, Patrick and Friel, 1972). In similar studies of worker preparation, Miller and Berenson (1976) found significant improvements in self-awareness, career awareness, decision-making, and placement skills for students of IPS-trained teacher-counselors.

In one of the earliest studies of worker performance, Truax and his associates (Truax, Leslie, Smith, Glenn and Fisher, 1967) assessed the relationship between the rehabilitation clients' perceived level of IPS offered by the vocational instructor and the clients' functioning during training. The researchers established a significant but low level of relationship with work progress, quality, attitudes, dependability, and cooperation. Again, it is remarkable for purposes of understanding the limited relationships that the vocational instructors had not been trained programmatically in IPS and the study relied upon the client's perception of level of IPS.

Studies of the effects of IPS-trained personnel on worker performance in medical and mental health settings yield positive results. IPS-skilled medical corpsmen were significantly more effective than when they were untrained in working with hospital patients (Anthony and Wain, 1971). Similarly, mental health worker use of "training as treatment" groups (Vitalo and Cohen, 1976; Evans and Vitalo, 1976) and client or helpee exploration but not process change (Vitalo, Vitalo, Brown and O'Donnell, 1976, 1977) improved significantly as a consequence of IPS training.

Table 5. Effects of Employers Upon Employees

STUDY				METHOD		RESULTS		
Nature	Authors	Dates	N of Population	Measures	Time	Treatment	Control	Diff
1) Worker Preparation	Myers, Thompson, et al.	1972	105 Secondary Students (12 Teacher/Counselors)	Occupational Action	1 year	5.0	3.9	*
				Quality Occupational Action	"	2.5	2.1	*
				Specific Occupational Information	"	5.6	3.9	*
				Career Information	"	3.4	1.9	*
				Sources Quantity Career	"	5.7	3.4	*
				Question Quantity Occupation	"	13.3	10.9	*
				Class Quantity Occ. Decisions	"	7.8	5.5	*
			(100 Secondary Students)	Time Talking/Participant	"	2.6	2.2	*
			(55 Secondary Students)	Certainty Vocational Choice	"	42%	12%	*
			(42 Secondary Students)	Grade Point Average	"	2.7	2.4	N.S.

Table 5. (Continued)

STUDY				METHOD		RESULTS		
Nature	Authors	Dates	N of Population	Measures	Time	Treatment	Control	Diff
			(48 Secondary Students)	Absenteeism	"	56% low	29% low	*
			(59 Secondary Students)	Vocational Maturity (C.D.I.)	"			*
2) Worker Preparation	Miller & Berenson	1976	528 Secondary Students (20 Staff)	Self-Awareness	1 year	+63% (2.67)		*
				Career Awareness	"	+79% (3.00)		*
				Career Decision	"	+67% (3.00)		*
				Career Placement	"	+79% (4.72)		*
3) Worker Performance	Truax, Leslie, et al.	1967	165 Youth (8 Staff)	Work Progress	1 mo.	.15		*
				Work Product	"	.04		N.S.
				Work Quality	"	.23		*
				Work Attitude	"	.18		*
				Dependability	"	.24		*
				Cooperation	"	.19		*
4) Worker Performance	Anthony & Wain	1971	100 Patients (15 Medical Corps.)	Work Ratings	6 mos.	5.1	4.0	*
				Effectiveness Ratings	"	85%	20%	*

Table 5. (Continued)

Nature	Authors	Dates	N of Population	Measures	Time	Treatment	Control	Diff
5) Worker Performance	Vitalo & Cohen	1976	11 Mental Health Workers (2 Trainers)	Use of Training as Treatment Groups	3 years "	1.71	.29	*
6) Worker Performance	Vitalo, Vitalo, et al.	1976 1977	43 Paraprof. (4 Supervisors)	Helper IPS Helper Changes Client Exploration Client Process Change		1.70 – 2.70 .26 – .33 2.52 63.6%	1.10 – 1.82 .07 – .11 1.64 55.5%	* * * N.S.
7) Worker Performance	Aspy & Roebuck	1976	257 Teachers (12 Principals)	School Climate School Setting Leadership Educational Practice School/Community Relations	1 year " " " "	784.80 50.70 43.82 44.91 49.05	701.20 45.35 39.22 40.14 42.02	* * * * *
8) Worker Performance	Aspy & Roebuck	1977	40 Teachers (1 Principal)	Accept Student Ideas Student Recall Facts Student Thinking Student Confusion	1 year " " "	2.55% 33.06% 13.33% 6.81%	0.61% 24.35% 5.56% 10.60%	* * * *

Column group headers: STUDY (Nature, Authors, Dates) | METHOD (N of Population, Measures, Time) | RESULTS (Treatment, Control, Diff)

Table 5. (Continued)

STUDY				METHOD		RESULTS		
Nature	Authors	Dates	N of Population	Measures	Time	Treatment	Control	Diff
9) Worker Performance	Aspy & Roebuck	1978	287 Teachers (12 Principals)	Work Variables	6 mos.	42	14 – 22	*
10) Worker Performance	Carkhuff	1971a	55 Unemployed (6 Empl. Trainers)	Work Placement Job Retention	6 mos. "	100% 88%		* *
11) Worker Performance	Bozarth & Rubin	1975	1,000 Clients (160 Counselors)	Vocational Gain $ Earned	6 mos. "			* *
12) Worker Performance	Pierce & Schauble	1970	30 Supervisees (10 Supervisors)	Supervisees Effect Supervisors Effect	6 mos. "			* *
13) Organization Productivity	Day, Methany, & Megathlin	1980	2,000 Inmates (150 Officers)	Idle Days $ Savings Accident Rate $ Savings	1 year " " "	31/day 7.5/day	66/day $59,568 15.1/day $59,000	* * * N/A
14) Organization Productivity	Collingwood Douds, et al	1978	15,000 Youth (14 Staff)	City-Wide Delinquency Juvenile Referrals Juvenile Court Return on Investment	6 years " " "	-3.9% -36% -12.5% +174%		* * * *

Table 5. (Continued)

Nature	Authors	Dates	N of Population	Measures	Time	Treatment	Control	Diff
						STUDY / METHOD	RESULTS	
15) Organization Productivity	Friel, Pierce, et al.	1983	10,000 Employees (645 Managers)	Skill Acquisition		3.5	2.0	1.5*
				OJT Application		96%		*
				OJT Improvement		95%		*
				OJT Transfer		90%		*
				$ Savings	9 mos.	$1,425,975		N/A
					1 year	$2,309,610		N/A
				Return on Investment	9 mos.	10:1		*
16) Organization Productivity	Brillinger & Friel	1981	750 Employees (55 Managers)	$ Savings	1 year	+100 – 600%		*
				Safety	"	$100,000		N/A
				Return on Investment	"	+500%		*
17) Organization Productivity	Feder	1982a	150 Employees (15 Supervisors)	% Quantity Outcome	2 mos.	53%		*
				$ Savings	"	$52,414		N/A
18) Organization Productivity	Feder	1982b	500 Employees (35 Managers)	Value	3 mos.	100%		*
				Skill Application	"	89%		*
				Specific Examples	"	71 – 77%		*
19) Organization Productivity	Shultz & Rowe	1982	650 Employees (40 Managers)	Skill Application	6 mos.	95%		*
				Quantity Application	"	55%		*
				$ Cost Avoidance	"	$400,913		N/A

61

Table 5. (Continued)

	STUDY		METHOD				RESULTS		
Nature	Authors	Dates	N of Population	Measures	Time	Treatment	Control	Diff	
20) Organization Productivity	Holder	1982	150 Employees (10 Managers)	Skill Application	3 mos.	90%		*	
				# Applications	"	22		N/A	
				$ Cost Avoidance	"	$12,962		N/A	
21) Organization Productivity	Douds	1982	2,000 Employees (181 Managers)	Skill Application	6 mos.	85%		*	
				Quantity Application	"	60%		*	
				$ Cost Avoidance	"	$252,065		N/A	
22) Organization Productivity	Pierce	1983	100 Employees (15 Supervisors)	Recognize Differences	6 mos.	3.83	2.67	*	
				Reflecting	"	3.62	2.20	*	
				Sharing Perceptions	"	3.59	2.36	*	
				Resolve Differences	"	3.44	2.44	*	
				Recognize Bias	"	4.00	2.38	*	
				Rec. Discrimination	"	3.95	2.60	*	
				Recognize Fairness	"	3.50	2.33	*	
				Plan Time	"	3.67	2.17	*	
				Plan Goals	"	4.07	2.52	*	
				Plan Action	"	3.92	2.52	*	
				Monitor Work	"	4.06	2.60	*	
				Analyze Staff	"	3.50	2.17	*	
				Make Assignments	"	3.85	2.49	*	

Table 5. (Concluded)

STUDY				METHOD			RESULTS		
Nature	Authors	Dates	*N* of Population	Measures	Time	Treatment	Control	Diff	
22) Organization Productivity (concluded)	Pierce	1983		Prepare Meeting	6 mos.	3.67	2.33	*	
				Conduct Discussions	"	3.74	2.56	*	
				Set Expectations	"	3.59	2.43	*	
				Monitor Performance	"	3.73	2.28	*	
				Motivate Performance	"	3.75	2.62	*	
				Time Savings	"	13,900 hrs.		N/A	
				$ Savings	"	$128,897		N/A	
				Return on Investment	"	3.24		N/A	

Aspy and his associates conducted a number of studies of the effects of IPS-trained employers on worker performance in school settings. They found that principals trained in IPS have teachers who create significantly better school climates and situations and manifest significantly better leadership, educational practices, and school-community relations (Aspy and Roebuck, 1976). IPS-trained principals also have teachers who demonstrate significantly more facilitation of student ideas, student recall of facts and thinking, and significantly less student silence and confusion (Aspy and Roebuck, 1977). In general, then, employees of high IPS-functioning administrators demonstrate significantly better work performance on a variety of work variables (Aspy and Roebuck, 1978).

Studies of the effects of IPS-trained employers on worker performance in work settings yield similar results. IPS-trained employment trainers drawn from the ranks of previously unemployed adults were able to place 100% of their trainees who, in turn, retained 88% of their jobs (Carkhuff, 1971b). On the other hand, 1,000 clients demonstrated significantly greater vocational gains and earnings for relatively higher (but untrained) IPS-functioning counselors than for relatively lower-functioning counselors (Bozarth and Rubin, 1975). Similarly, the supervisees of relatively higher (but untrained) IPS-functioning supervisors evidenced significantly more IPS than those of relatively lower-functioning supervisors (Pierce and Schauble, 1970).

Together, these studies of worker performance suggest that there is a human or interpersonal dimension to all work performance. This dimension is usually passed on from the manager or supervisor to the supervisee or worker. Good supervision of worker performance relates the worker's frame of reference to the tasks at hand.

In this context, managerial and supervisory IPS have been related to organizational productivity. In the General Dynamics studies, the IPS training program formed the nucleus of all worker performance and agency productivity programs (Friel, Pierce, Cannon, Feder, Holder and Shultz, 1982; Holder and Shultz, 1982; Holder, Schultz, Feder, Pierce and Friel, 1982). The IPS management training program was summarized by "Get-Give-Merge and Go": get the supervisee's image of the task; give your image of the task; merge or converge the images; go to work to implement the task. This IPS-based approach contrasts vividly with the usual "Give and Go" approach of management and supervision. The estimated dollar savings of such an efficient management approach ranged in the millions of dollars.

Other studies of organizational productivity have related employer IPS to agency productivity by assessing a variety of productivity measures: skill applications (Douds, 1982; Feder, 1982a, 1982b, 1983; Holder, 1982a, 1983; Schultz and Rowe, 1982); time and dollar savings (Brillinger and Friel, 1981; Douds, 1982; Feder, 1982a, 1983; Holder, 1982, 1983; Shultz and Rowe, 1982); idle days, accident, and safety savings (Blakeman, 1980; Brillinger and Friel, 1981; Day, Methany and Megathlin, 1982, 1980; Megathlin, 1969a, 1969b; Megathlin and Day, 1972; Shultz and Rowe, 1982) and system benefits and return-on-investment (Brillinger and Friel, 1981; Collingwood, 1982).

Perhaps one of the most significant of all of these studies is the study of supervision conducted by Pierce (1983). Pierce trained supervisors in all of the traditional supervisory "survival" skills: planning, organizing, and directing as well as problem solving, controlling, and appraising work. In addition, he trained the supervisors in interpersonal skills and other organizational skills involving eliminating bias and providing equal opportunity. Pierce found significant improvement in skill development and application as well as important cost-avoidance savings and return-on-investment. Perhaps most important, Pierce found that 80% of the supervisory personnel found the interpersonal skills most productive while the remaining skills ranked no higher than 33%: planning skills, 33%; performance discussion skills, 27%; controlling work and assignment-making skills, 20%. The greatest productivity gains accrued to those supervisors who used their interpersonal skills to communicate about work procedures and who then devised methods to improve the work procedures.

In summary, the effects of employer IPS on worker performance and agency productivity is well documented. All 22 studies (100%) and 80 of 83 applicable indices (96%) established positive results. Again, with the exception of the Truax, Bozarth, and Pierce studies, all of the studies involved systematic training calculated to directly affect the outcome indices.

7   The Effects of the Direct Training of Recipients

In 1964, the first systematic recipient training programs were introduced. Instead of training professional or lay helpers who, in turn, offered their helping skills to the recipients, it was concluded that the direct training of recipients was a "preferred model of treatment" (Carkhuff, 1966, 1969, 1971a, 1971b; Carkhuff and Berenson, 1967, 1976). These programs gave birth to a multitude of IPS-based programs (Carkhuff and Berenson, 1976) and, later still, behaviorally oriented social skills training programs. (The latter will not be reviewed within the purview of this study.) Thus, recipients were taught to help themselves. Whereas the studies of the effects of helpers upon recipients emphasized the IPS of the helpers, the direct training of recipients involved the IPS of the recipients. Children, counselees, learners, and employees were trained directly in IPS and other skills needed to function effectively in their living, learning, and working environments.

Living Outcomes

The 35 living outcome studies of the effects of the direct training of recipients may be found in Table 6. The living outcome studies emphasize child, youth, and adult behavior and adjustment. The N's of the recipient populations range from 6 to 695 with a total of 2,279 recipients involved. The measures emphasize incidents of pathological behavior and its recidivism or repetition. The time at which the measurements were taken range from immediate to three years following the training intervention.

In one of the earliest studies of "training as treatment" for family adjustment, Carkhuff and Bierman (1970) trained parents to help their own emotionally disturbed children. While these researchers obtained IPS changes in the parents, they did not achieve differences in either the constructive personality change of the parents or the children. At this point, it was concluded that "you get what you train for."

Table 6. Direct Training of Helpees

STUDY				METHOD		RESULTS		
Nature	Authors	Dates	N of Population	Measures	Time	Treatment	Control	Diff
1) Family Adjustment	Carkhuff & Bierman	1970	21 Parents	IPS Constructive Change Child Adjustment	3 mos. " "	2.9	1.5	* Neg. Neg.
2) Family Adjustment	Griffin & Carkhuff	1976	10 Children (5 Parents)	Behavior Problems	6 mos.	1.5/mo.	1/day	*
3) Family Adjustment	Valle & Marinelli	1975	30 Adults	Interpersonal Relating	6 mos.			*
4) Family Adjustment	Bopp & Chapados	1978	32 Adults	# Fights Goal Attainment	6 mos. "			*
5) Family Adjustment	Santantonio & Vitalo	1977	8 Adults	IPS Acquisition IPS Application Marital Success Outcome Goals Sexual Relations	6 mos. " " " "	4.03 3.77 3.58 3.88 1.92	2.10 2.40 2.39 1.63 1.75	* * * * N.S.

The Effects of the Direct Training of Recipients

Table 6. (Continued)

STUDY				METHOD		RESULTS		
Nature	Authors	Dates	N of Population	Measures	Time	Treatment	Control	Diff
6) Family Adjustment	Shores & Vitalo	1977a	8 Adults	IPS Acquisition IPS Application Marital Success	6 mos. " "	2.63 3.60 3.59	1.65 2.63 1.00	* * *
7) Family Adjustment	Davison	1976a	46 Parents	Leveling Understanding Self-Esteem Self-Realization Transcendence	3 mos. " " " "	4.19 3.93 352.60 98.50 111.40	3.11 2.97 345.00 95.60 105.80	* * * * *
8) Family Adjustment	Davidson	1976b	101 Parents	Social Needs Respect for Others Self-Realization	3 mos. " "	2.45 3.95 4.00	1.84 3.42 2.59	* * *
9) Family Adjustment	Finkelman	1976	100 Parents	Dogmatism Belonging Self-Concept Inner Direction Life Purpose	3 mos. " " " "	-29.80 1.36 342.72 85.50 103.20	-21.77 1.75 333.19 90.70 109.40	* * * * *

Table 6. (Continued)

STUDY			METHOD			RESULTS		
Nature	Authors	Dates	N of Population	Measures	Time	Treatment	Control	Diff
10) Family Adjustment	Finkelman & Simister	1976	19 Parents	Empathy	3 mos.	2.34	1.62	*
				Respect	"	3.87	2.96	*
				Experiencing	"	4.02	2.39	*
				Dogmatism	"	-31.60	-25.40	*
				Belonging	"	1.63	1.63	*
				Self-Concept	"	336.70	318.90	*
				Inner Direction	"	86.50	79.00	*
				Life Purpose	"	104.90	96.60	*
11) Family Adjustment	Simister	1976a	51 Parents	Dogmatism	3 mos.	-22.76	-16.61	N.S.
				Belonging	"	1.27	1.53	N.S.
				Self-Concept	"	338.96	336.00	*
				Inner Direction	"	88.28	84.02	*
				Life Purpose	"	110.41	105.75	*
				Empathy	"	2.46	1.86	*
				Respect	"	3.99	3.44	*
				Experiencing	"	3.92	2.58	*

The Effects of the Direct Training of Recipients

Table 6. (Continued)

STUDY				METHOD			RESULTS		
Nature	Authors	Dates	N of Population	Measures	Time	Treatment	Control	Diff	
12) Family Adjustment	Simister	1976b	50 Parents	Dogmatism	3 mos.	-36.70	-26.82	*	
				Belonging	"	1.44	1.98	*	
				Self-Concept	"	346.56	330.32	*	
				Inner Direction	"	93.20	86.92	*	
				Life Purpose	"	108.24	100.56	*	
				Empathy	"	2.45	1.83	*	
				Respect	"	3.91	3.41	*	
				Experiencing	"	4.09	2.59	*	
13) Family Adjustment	Leonidas	1976a	22 Parents	Self-Criticism	3 mos.	39.10	38.40	N.S.	
				Identity	"	122.10	117.60	*	
				Self-Satisfaction	"	111.10	103.70	*	
				Behavior	"	112.10	106.00	*	
				Physical Self	"	66.80	63.40	*	
				Moral Self	"	72.30	70.30	N.S.	
				Personal Self	"	67.10	62.00	*	
				Family Self	"	68.80	65.10	*	
				Social Self	"	70.30	66.60	*	
				Total	"	345.00	327.00	*	

Table 6. (Continued)

STUDY				METHOD			RESULTS		
Nature	Authors	Dates	N of Population	Measures	Time	Treatment	Control	Diff	
14) Family Adjustment	Davison	1976c	20 Parents	Self-Concept	3 mos.	347.30	333.95	*	
				Self-Realization	"	100.35	97.49	*	
				Transcendence	"	109.60	105.95	N.S.	
				Social Needs	"	2.53	2.39	*	
				Respect from Others	"	4.02	4.01	N.S.	
				Self-Realization	"	3.96	3.34	*	
15) Youth Adjustment	Leonidas	1976b	41 Children	General Anxiety	3 mos.	17.15	19.05	Neg.	
			15 Children	Self-Anxiety	"	8.40	7.07	N.S.	
			" "	Popularity	"	9.07	7.73	*	
			" "	Behavior	"	14.70	12.50	*	
			" "	Intellectual	"	13.80	13.60	N.S.	
			" "	Physical Appearance	"	9.40	9.07	N.S.	
			" "	Happiness	"	8.20	6.93	*	
			" "	Overall Self	"	61.33	55.60	N.S.	

Table 6. (Continued)

The Effects of the Direct Training of Recipients

| STUDY | | | | METHOD | | RESULTS | | |
Nature	Authors	Dates	N of Population	Measures	Time	Treatment	Control	Diff
16) Youth Adjustment	Berenson, Carkhuff & Myrus	1966	36 Youth	Tape IPS	2 mos.	2.70	1.76 – 1.88	*
				Tape Explore	"	2.67	1.48 – 1.74	*
				Interview Report	"			*
				Self-Report	"			*
				Significant Others	"			*
17) Youth Adjustment	Cabush & Edwards	1976	20 Clients	Self-Help Response	6 wks.	2.95	1.70	*
				Self-Ratings	"	4.70	4.30	N.S.
				Other Ratings	"	4.80	3.50	*
				Self-Goal Achievement	"	4.40	4.20	N.S.
				Other Goal Achievement	"	4.30	3.20	*
18) Youth Achievement	Maloney & Chapados	1978a	6 Youth	Lying (per week)	1 year	2.80	13.60	*
				Stealing (per week)	"	1.00	3.20	*
				Manipulation (per week)	"	4.30	10.30	*
				Relating Problems (per month)	"	2.00	7.90	*
				Empathy	"	3.78	1.00	*

Table 6. (Continued)

Nature	Authors	Dates	N of Population	Measures	Time	Treatment	Control	Diff
	STUDY			METHOD		RESULTS		
19) Youth Adjustment	Rankin, Chapados & Gorbette	1980	22 Youth	# Conflicts	5 mos.	1/19 days	1/21 days	*
20) Youth Adjustment	Shores & Vitalo	1977b	9 Handicapped Youth	IPS / Regular Class	6 mos. / "	1.97 – 2.39 / 71%	1.28 / 0	* / *
21) Youth Adjustment	Devine	1977	300 Delinquent Youth	Recidivism	1 year	9%	25 – 50%	*
22) Youth Adjustment	Devine	1977	200 Delinquent Youth	Recidivism	1 year	5%	23 – 50%	*
23) Patient Adjustment	Devine	1977	25 Ex-Offenders	Recidivism	1 year	)	30%	*
24) Patient Adjustment	Bellingham & Devine	1977	40 Ex-Offenders	Recidivism	4 mos.	20%	70%	*
25) Patient Adjustment	Bellingham & Devine	1977	21 Drug Rehab. Patients	Recidivism / Employment	4 mos. / "	0% / 63%	6% / 42%	* / *

The Effects of the Direct Training of Recipients

Table 6. (Continued)

STUDY			METHOD			RESULTS		Diff
Nature	Authors	Dates	N of Population	Measures	Time	Treatment	Control	
26) Patient Adjustment	Devine, Bellingham, et al.	1977 1981	695 Ex-Offenders	Recidivism $ Savings	2 yrs. "	30% $620,000	60% $1,042,000 $522,000	* N/A
27) Patient Adjustment	Montgomery	1977	78 Ex-Offenders	% Complete % Escape % Re-arrest % Place	3 mos. " " "	93.6% 2.6% 0 100%		* * * *
28) Patient Adjustment	Griffin	1976	48 Ex-Offenders	Recidivism Drug Usage Placement	1 year " "	7% 0% 100%	40% 60% 30%	* * *
29) Patient Adjustment	Pierce, Schauble & Wilson	1971	16 Clients	Empathy Internalize Combined Processes	Immed. " "	3.4 3.3 3.1	2.1 – 2.2 1.5 – 2.6 2.0 – 2.3	* * *
30) Patient Adjustment	Pierce & Drasgow	1969	35 Patients	IPS Discharge	1 mo. 1 year	2.53 71%	1.14 – 1.55 42%	* *

Table 6. (Continued)

STUDY				METHOD		RESULTS		
Nature	Authors	Dates	N of Population	Measures	Time	Treatment	Control	Diff
31) Patient Adjustment	Vitalo	1971	29 Patients	IPS Tape IPS Live Ward Behavior Clinical Pathology	1 mo. " " "	2.30 – 2.35 2.42 – 2.47 80%	1.12 – 1.31 1.26 – 1.56 20 – 22%	* * * Neg.
32) Patient Adjustment	Bopp, Bushee & Chapados	1978a	19 Patients	Depressive Periods Period Length	1 year "			* *
33) Patient Adjustment	Chapados, Riehl & Peterson	1978	19 Patients	Thought Disorders	Immed.	3.98 (of 5)	1.40 (of 5)	*
34) Patient Adjustment	Vitalo & Cohen	1976	14 Patients	IPS Living Success	1 year "	3.20 3.10	1.40 2.00	* *

Table 6. (Concluded)

STUDY				METHOD				RESULTS		
Nature	Authors	Dates	N of Population	Measures	Time		Treatment	Control	Diff
35) Patient Adjustment	Vitalo & Ross	1977	88 Patients	Skills Learned	1 year		80%	35%	*
				Mean # Skills	"		1.62	.38	*
				Symptom Benefits	"		4.05	3.97	N.S.
				Employment	"		38%	21%	*
				Weeks Worked	"		8.93	5.14	*
				New Friends	"		83%	50%	*
				New Activities	"		1.38	.34	*

Additional generalization benefits are serendipitous. In this context, Griffin and Carkhuff (1976) found that they were able to reduce significantly the behavior problems of children by directly training them and their parents to apply IPS skills. A number of subsequent studies established significant benefits on a variety of indices: interpersonal relating (Santantonio and Vitalo, 1977; Shores and Vitalo, 1977a; Valle and Marinelli, 1975), reduction of fights (Bopp and Chapados, 1978), achievement of goals (Bopp, Bushee and Cahapdos, 1978b; Santantonio and Vitalo, 1977), and achievement of marital success (Shores and Vitalo, 1977a; Santantonio and Vitalo, 1977).

In the most extensive series of studies on parent training, Bierman and his associates (1976) employed a variety of indices in assessing outcome. Davison (1976b, 1976c, 1976d) demonstrated the efficacy of IPS-based training on the parental self-concepts, needs, and realization. Finkelman (1976) and Finkelman and Simister (1976) showed the relationship of parent training to indices of dogmatism, belonging, inner-direction, and life purpose as well as empathy, respect, and experiencing. Simister (1976a, 1976b) demonstrated the positive effects of both staff and trained community leaders on indices of dogmatism, inner-directedness, and life purpose as well as empathy, respect, and experiencing. Leonidas (1976a) demonstrated the effects of IPS-based parent training on indices of parental physical, personal, family, and social self-concepts as well as behavior and satisfaction. In addition, Leonidas (1976b) also demonstrated the effects of the direct training of youth in IPS-based programs on indices of popularity, happiness, and behavior, while obtaining a negative relationship with general anxiety.

In studies of youth and young adult behavior, it was found that significant differences were affected in a variety of living outcome indices: interpersonal relations, especially with "significant others" (Berenson, Carkhuff and Myrus, 1966); self-help responses and interpersonal and goal behaviors (Cabush and Edwards, 1976); lying, stealing, manipulating, relating, and empathizing (Maloney and Chapados, 1978a); the number of conflicts between roommates (Rankin, Chapados and Gorbette, 1980); and the IPS and regular class placements of handicapped youth (Shores and Vitalo, 1977b). In all of these studies, the authors trained for the outcome measures they desired to affect. In the Cabush and Edwards study, however, they did not obtain differences in self-ratings of interpersonal and goal behavior functioning. The accuracy of the perceptions of all subjects in all studies continues to appear to be a function of their levels of functioning: the lower they function, the more distorted their perceptions (Cannon and Carkhuff, 1969).

Several studies established significant reductions in recidivism and improvements in employment for ex-offenders. Bellingham and associates (1977a, 1977b, 1978a, 1978b), Devine and associates (1976, 1977, 1978, 1981), Montgomery (1977) and Griffin (1976) all reduced recidivism and improved employment by training the ex-offenders in IPS and other life skills. Basically, what these researchers did was to assess the kinds of IPS requirements that would be needed by the ex-offenders upon returning to their living, learning, and working environments. Then they designed and delivered the IPS programs to meet those needs. In the process, some of these programs established substantial dollar savings due to the ex-offenders' productivity (Devine, Bellingham, Essex and Steinberg, 1977, 1981). In these days of escalating recidivism rates, the recidivism rates ranging from 2% to 30% are particularly noteworthy.

In terms of patient adjustment, Pierce and Drasgow (1969) found training patients to be the preferred mode of treatment. Using medicinal, individual, and group treatment and control conditions, the authors found that training patients in IPS was significantly more effective than all other treatment and control conditions. They found these results immediately in interpersonal functioning and, upon follow-up, in hospital discharge rates.

Vitalo (1971) incorporated group therapy and non-specific treatment controls in studying IPS. He found that systematic IPS training was nearly six times more effective than modeling in group therapy in demonstrating neuropsychiatric patients' improvement in interpersonal functioning, Moreover, the IPS acquired in training were employed by the patients in their ward relationships outside of the immediate group setting. However, while there was evidence for the patients' improved social functioning, the relationship with the patients' clinical pathology and anxiety levels was negative. Again, you get what you train for.

In this regard, working with simple, straightforward IPS training programs leading directly to specific treatment goals, Chapados and his associates were able to reduce neuropsychiatric patient pathology: depressive periods and period lengths (Bopp, Bushee and Chapados, 1978a) and irrational thought disorders (Chapados, Riehl and Peterson, 1978). Finally, Vitalo related IPS training to success in living (1978) and a variety of other living outcome measures: number and type of skills learned; employment and weeks worked; new friends and activities. However, they obtained non-significant results from the relationship with symptom benefits (Vitalo and Ross, 1977). Training is the preferred mode of treatment for specific, operational goals.

In summary, the effects of the direct training of helpees are demonstrated. Only three of the 35 studies did not produce predominantly positive results. Thus, 32 of the 35 studies (91%) were predominantly positive while 108 of the 128 indices (85%) assessed yielded positive outcomes.

Again, systematic IPS training appeared to be a critical source of effect in the living outcomes of the helpees. Where the results were mixed, the goals were mixed (i.e., the training programs were not developed and implemented systematically to achieve all of the goals involved). In this regard, with the exception of Bierman's associates, none of the studies emphasized systematic follow-up or environmental support programs other than for purposes of evaluation.

Learning Outcomes

The 26 learning outcome studies reflecting the effects of the direct training of learners may be found in Table 7. The learning outcome studies emphasize youth and adult development. The *N*'s of the learner populations range from 7 to 1,353 with a total of 3,610 learners involved. The measures emphasize the physical, emotional, and intellectual functioning of the learners as well as related indices of their effects. The time at which the measurements were taken ranges from one month to one year following the training intervention.

Studies of youth development based on an IPS training core yield improved functioning on a variety of physical, emotional-interpersonal, and intellectual indices. Thus, Berenson and associates (1978) trained inner city "fall-outs" (youth too young to drop out) in IPS, fitness, and learning skills. They obtained significant growth, including nearly one and one-half years on the Iowa Achievement Test for reading. Finally, they demonstrated a 95% school return rate in 3 months.

Carkhuff and his associates (1974) trained institutionalized delinquent youth in IPS and other skills and got more than one and one-half years of growth on the California Achievement Test (CAT) for reading and math and a 56% reduction in elopement or runaways. Collingwood and his associates (1976, 1978) trained delinquent

The Effects of the Direct Training of Recipients

Table 7. Direct Training of Learners

| STUDY | | | | METHOD | | RESULTS | | |
Nature	Authors	Dates	N of Population	Measures	Time	Treatment	Control	Diff
1) Youth Development	Berenson, Berenson, et al.	1978	152 Dropouts	Physical (Fitness) Emotional (IPS) Intellectual (Iowa) School Return	3 mos. " " "	4.61 3.66 7.47 Gr. 95%	3.89 2.67 6.08 Gr.	* * * *
2) Youth Development	Carkhuff, Devine, et al.	1974	120 Youth	Physical (AAPHER) Emotional (IPS) Intellectual (CAT) Runaways	1 year " " "	69% 2.8% 7.6 Gr. 12%	46% 1.4% 6.1 Gr. 28%	* * * *
3) Youth Development	Collingwood, Douds, et al.	1976 1978	887 Youth	Physical (Fitness) Emotional (IPS) Intellectual (Learn) Intellectual (Study) Recidivism	2.5 yrs. " " " "	3.00 2.70 2.60 2.90 10.7%	2.50 1.50 1.60 2.00 45.5%	* * * * *
4) Youth Development	Hall	1978a	25 Youth	Physical (Run/Flex/Sit) Emotional (Decisions + IPS) Intellectual (CAT) Recidivism	1 year " 6 mos. 1 year	3.80 3.10 +6.2 mos. 28%	2.70 2.10 +6 mos. 50%	* * N.S. *

IPS: Interpersonal Skills and Human Productivity

Table 7. (Continued)

Nature	Authors	Dates	N of Population	Measures	Time	Treatment	Control	Diff
5) Youth Development	Hall	1978b	55 Youth	Physical (Fitness)	6 mos.	2.50	2.00	*
				Emotional (IPS)	"	3.00	1.50	*
				Intellectual (CAT)	"	+2.7 yrs.		*
				Recidivism	"	12%	26%	*
6) Youth Development	Carkhuff	1971b	10 Youth	Physical (Fitness)	2 mos.	2.50	2.00	*
				Emotional (IPS)	"	2.20	1.40	*
				Intellectual (Progress)	"	3.00	1.50	*
				School Crisis	"	1/mo.	1/day	*
7) Youth Development	Danley, Ahearn, & Battenschlag	1975	270 Learning Deficit Youth	Math Homework	6 mos.	+ 66%		*
				Reading Homework	"	+ 37%		*
				School Homework	"	+ 23%		*
				School Talk at Home	"	+ 55%		*
				Parent-Initiated to School	"	+ 52%		*
				Parent-Initiated Visits	"	+ 48%		*
				Discipline Problems	"	−31%		*

Table 7. (Continued)

Nature	Authors	Dates	N of Population	Measures	Time	Treatment	Control	Diff
						RESULTS		
	STUDY			METHOD				
8) Youth Development	Devine, Bellingham, et al.	1977	10 Delinquent Youth	Physical (Fitness)	6 mos.	3.00–3.80	2.30 – 3.10	*
				Behavioral:				
				Self & Other Care	"	2.70–3.10	1.70–3.40	*
				Responsible	"	1.70–2.90	1.40–3.00	*
				Interpersonal Behavior	"	1.30–2.90	2.10–3.20	*
				Intellectual:				
				Reading	"	7.90	6.70	*
				Spelling	"	5.50	5.00	*
				Math	"	5.00	4.50	*
				Runaway	"	3.00	23.00	*
9) Youth Development	Evans & Vitalo	1981	7 Youth	Grade Point Average	4 mos.	3.34–3.60	2.46	*
10) Youth Development	Rutledge & Holder	1982	162 Secondary Students	Reading (with Work)	6 wks.	+ 2.5 Gr.		*
11) Youth Development	Aspy, et al.	1982	40 Elementary Students	Stanford Achievement	1 year	2.0 Gr.	1.0 Gr.	*

Table 7. (Continued)

| STUDY | | | | METHOD | | RESULTS | | |
Nature	Authors	Dates	N of Population	Measures	Time	Treatment	Control	Diff
12) Youth Development	Carkhuff & Griffin	1970	21 Youth	Present Ratings	1 mo.	4.0 (of 5)	1.0 (of 5)	*
13) Youth Development	Chapados & Maloney	1978	16 Youth	Disruptive Behavior	3 mos.	1/42 min.	1/18 min.	*
14) Youth Development	Cohen, Cashwell, et al.	1976	60 Elementary Students	Student Decency Student Change	3 mos. "	4.10 3.75	3.85	* N/A
15) Youth Development	Wawrykow	1978	95 Elementary Students	IPS	3 mos.			*
16) Youth Development	Steinberg, Bellingham & Devine	1981	50 Ex-Offenders	Physical (Fitness) Emotional (IPS) Intellectual (Read) Intellectual (Math) Recidivism	3 mos. " " " "	3.00 2.70 + 1.30 Gr. + 3.50 Gr. 31%	1.80 1.50 + .20 Gr. + .20 Gr. 80%	* * * * *

Table 7. (Continued)

STUDY				METHOD				RESULTS		
Nature	Authors	Dates	N of Population	Measures	Time		Treatment	Control	Diff
17) Adult Development	Carkhuff	1971a	14 Human Resource Specialists	Physical (Fitness)	6 mos.		3.50	2.00	*
				Emotional (IPS)	"		3.20	1.50	*
				Intellectual (Progress)	"		4.50	1.50	*
				Student Ratings	"		4.30–4.70		N/A
				Staff Ratings	"		3.50–3.60		N/A
18) Adult Development	Carkhuff	1971a	22 Trainers	Physical (Fitness)	6 mos.		3.30	1.50	*
				Emotional (IPS)	"		3.30	1.40	*
				Intellectual (Progress)	"		4.20	1.50	*
				Work Place	"		100%		N/A
19) Adult Development	Carkhuff	1971a	26 Officers	Physical (Fitness)	1 mo.		3.00	2.40	*
				Emotional (IPS)	"		2.60	1.40	*
				Intellectual (Progress)	"		3.00	2.10	*
				Effects on Helpers	"		2.30	1.40	*
20) Adult Development	Carkhuff	1971a	54 Parents, Teachers, and Administrators	Physical (Fitness)	2 mos.		2.50	1.50	*
				Emotional (IPS)	"		2.30	1.60	*
				Intellectual (Progress)	"		2.80	1.70	*
				Support	"		100%		N/A

Table 7. (Continued)

Nature	STUDY Authors	Dates	N of Population	METHOD Measures	Time	RESULTS Treatment	Control	Diff
21) Adult Development	Jeter, Phillips, et al	1975	35 Teachers	Physical (Fitness)	1 week	3.20–4.00	2.70–3.10	*
				Human (Communic.)	"	3.90	1.70	*
				Human (Discrim.)	"	.50	.80	*
				Educational	"	4.00	4.00	*
				Career	"	1.90	1.90	*
22) Adult Development	Battenschlag, Ahearn, et al.	1974	11 Teachers	IPS	10 mos.	41.20	16.00	*
				Education Skills	"	166.00	83.90	*
				Career Skills	"	37.30		N/A
23) Adult Development	Battenschlag, Ahearn, et al.	1974	8 Teacher Trainers	IPS	10 mos.	+ 25.20		*
				Education Skills	"	+ 82.10		*
				Career Skills	"	37.5		N/A
24) Adult Development	Roebuck	1982	83 Teachers	% Goal Achievement	1 mo.	95%		N/A
				% Student Mastery	"	92%		N/A

Table 7. (Concluded)

STUDY				METHOD			RESULTS		
Nature	Authors	Dates	N of Population	Measures	Time	Treatment	Control	Diff
25) Adult Development	Keeling	1979	11 Child Care Workers	IPS	5 mos.	2.90	1.60	*
				Decision Making Skills	"	4.50	1.70	*
				Program Devel. Skills	"	4.30	2.70	*
				Preparatory Ratings	"	4.00–4.50		N/A
				Products	"	1.00		N/A
26) Adult Development	Vitalo & Cohen	1977	22 Graduate Students	% Knowledge Acquisition	3 days	3.35	2.04–2.24	*
				Skill Application	"	58%	36%	*

87

youth in a diversion project and achieved significant physical, emotional, and intellectual growth, including in particular, learning and study skills as well as a recidivism rate of 10.7% against a base rate of 45.5% for control conditions.

Hall produced two important studies of intellectual improvement and recidivism reduction using IPS training as his core program. In the first study, he demonstrated non-significant intellectual growth of 6.2 months versus 6 months for the controls, but reduced the recidivism rate to 28% for six months (1978a). In the second study, he demonstrated 2.7 years CAT growth in one year and reduced recidivism by 48% (1978b).

In turn, a number of researchers trained youth to handle special problem areas in addition to physical, emotional, and intellectual development: school crises (Carkhuff, 1971b); school assignments, parent involvement, and disciplinary problems (Danley, Ahearn and Battenschlag, 1975; Document Development, Inc., 1979); behavioral responsibilities and runaways (Devine, Bellingham, Essex, and Steinberg, 1977); special reading difficulties in conjunction with work experiences (Rutledge and Holder, 1979, in Holder, 1982); achievement test results (Aspy, Aspy and Roebuck, 1982); presentations (Carkhuff and Griffin, 1970); disruptive behavior (Chapados and Maloney, 1978); and youth decency and change (Cohen, Cashwell, Phillips, Holder, Cook, Ellis, Greenberg and Renz, 1976).

In most of these studies, the youth demonstrated significant gains in physical, emotional, and intellectual functioning and in some external index of behavior change or gain. In all instances, IPS training constituted the core of the training program.

In this context, Wawrykow (1978) conducted a most revealing study in which he trained children in IPS employing a variety of learning models: the IPS-based human resource development (HRD) model; operant conditioning; social learning; and aversive control. He found that learning was most effective when the HRD model was present, thus emphasizing the learners' exploring, understanding, and acting.

In studies of young adult development, Steinberg, Bellingham, and Devine (1981) trained inmates in physical and learning skills as well as IPS. They obtained 1.3 years of reading growth and 3.5 years of math growth in a two-month program. Three-year follow-up data yielded a 31% rate of recidivism against a base rate of 80% for that population in that state.

Carkhuff (1971a) incorporated the direct training of learners in studies of a variety of adult populations: adult human relations specialists demonstrated significant gains in school programming and student and staff ratings; adult employment trainers demonstrated significant gains in training programming and work placement; adult officers demonstrated gains in helping programming and helping effectiveness; parents, teachers, administrators, and police officers demonstrated gains in school programming skills and school crisis reduction support. In all instances, the programs involved IPS skills directed toward specific problems or goals.

Finally, a number of researchers worked with teachers in direct training applications with a variety of indices. In addition to physical, interpersonal, and other HRD measures, the indices included: career skills (Battenschlag, et al., 1974); goal achievement and student mastery (Roebuck, 1978, in Aspy, Aspy and Roebuck, 1982); teaching preparation and product development (Keeling, 1979); and knowledge acquisition and skill application (Vitalo and Cohen, 1977).

In summary, the evidence for the direct training of learners is clear. All 26 studies (100%) and 77 of 78 applicable indices (99%) yielded positive results. The one instance of non-significant differences involved the training school data for intellectual functioning which was not significantly different from anticipated functioning for non-delinquent school youth (Hall, 1978a).

Again, systematic training of learners in IPS appeared to be a critical source of effect in the physical, emotional, and intellectual development of the learners. None of the programs involved systematic follow-ups or environmental supports.

Working Outcomes

Table 8 demonstrates the 27 working outcome studies of the effects of the direct training of employees. The working outcome studies emphasize worker placement and performance. The N's range from 5 to 5,697 with a total of 12,235. The measures include career skills and quantity and quality of performance. The time at which the measurements were taken ranges from immediate to 13 years following the training intervention.

Studies of preparing youth for employment support the effects of IPS-based career skills training on a variety of career activities: career awareness and expanding, career narrowing and decision making, career planning and placement, career maturation and plan

Table 8. Direct Training of Workers

STUDY			METHOD				RESULTS		
Nature	Authors	Dates	N of Population	Measures	Time	Treatment	Control	Diff
1) Worker Preparation	Tyler	1972	300 Secondary Students	Career Expand	1 year			*
				Career Narrow	"			*
				Career Plan	"			*
				Career Inadequacies	"			*
				Career Confusion	"			*
2) Worker Preparation	Friel, Berenson, et al.	1974	300 Secondary Students	Career Expand	1 year			*
				Career Narrow	"			*
				Career Preparation	"			*
				Career Mature	"			*
				Parent Involvement	"			*
3) Worker Preparation	Inman & Harberts	1976	234 Secondary Students	Cluster Awareness	3 years	7.08	1.82–2.34	*
				Self-Awareness	"	8.65	1.32–1.82	*
				Self/Job Awareness	"	2.57	.34–.55	*
				Job Req. Awareness	"	4.11	.21–.35	*
				Decision Making	"	14.62	2.81–3.38	*
				Career Plan	"	7.86	.71–2.63	*
				Job Information	"	3.39	.94–1.79	*
				Resume	"	2.53	.80–1.10	*
				Job Application	"	8.14	1.67–3.18	*
				Interview	"	3.30	.93–.51	*

Table 7. (Continued)

The Effects of the Direct Training of Recipients

Nature	Authors	Dates	N of Population	Measures	Time	Treatment	Control	Diff
	STUDY			**METHOD**		**RESULTS**		
4) Worker Preparation	Danley	1980	5,697 Youth	Career Awareness	1 year	4.06	10.00	*
				Career Decision	"	2.51	13.27	**
				Career Planning	"	2.00	8.57	*
				Finding Jobs	"	3.27–3.84	5.86–8.05	*
				Interview	"	3.79	7.96	*
				Revise Plan	"	1.44	4.74	*
				Cost Per Pupil	"	$51.45		
5) Worker Preparation	Jeter, Phillips, et al	1975	23 Secondary Students	Employment Selection	3 mos.	75%	9%	*
				Student Appearance	"	3.67–4.25	2.80–3.20	*
				Student Behavior	"	3.83–4.33	2.89–3.00	*
				Student Personality	"	4.00–4.17	2.90–3.11	*
				Student Interest	"	3.00	2.40	*
				Student Feedback	"	2.90	2.50	*
				Student Organization	"	2.90	1.90	*
				Student Performance	"	3.42	2.50	*
				Student Attendance	"	3.04	2.32	*
				Verbal Interaction	"	14.08	12.18	*
				Student Responsibility	"	2.08	1.51	*

Table 8. (Continued)

Nature	Authors	Dates	N of Population	Measures	Time	Treatment	Control	Diff
					STUDY / **METHOD** / **RESULTS**			
6) Worker Preparation	Lumley	1976	18 Manpower Students	Safety	3 mos.	9.61	4.56	*
				Belonging	"	2.00	2.61	N.S.
				Self-Esteem	"	310.61	291.56	*
				Self-Realization	"	84.59	76.06	*
				Transcendence	"	90.06	82.50	*
				Social Needs	"	2.07	1.62	*
				Respect from Others	"	3.28	2.85	*
				Self-Realization	"	3.55	2.50	*
7) Worker Preparation	Holder & Friel	1972	530 Youth	Work Experience	1 year	100%		*
				Related Career	"	42%		N/A
				Incentive Pay	"	7%		N/A
8) Worker Preparation	Holder, Friel & Tyler	1979	40 Youth	Quantity Career Skills	1 year	2.00	1.60	*
				Quality Career Skills	"	2.00	1.40	*
9) Worker Preparation	Holder & Mallory	1979	119 Youth	Quantity Employment Skills	1 year	2.50	1.80	*
				Quality Employment Skills	"	1.50	1.20	*

Table 8. (Continued)

STUDY				METHOD			RESULTS		
Nature	Authors	Dates	N of Population	Measures	Time	Treatment	Control	Diff	
10) Worker Preparation	Friel, Holder, & Franckowiak	1979	191 Youth	Coping Skills	1 year	1.70	1.40	*	
11) Worker Preparation	Friel, Holder, & Mallory	1979	99 Youth	Vocational Skills	1 year	2.70	1.30	*	
12) Worker Preparation	Friel, Franckowiak & Holder	1979	240 Youth	Dropouts Employee Placement	1 year "	3% 95.8%	20% 65–83%	* *	
13) Worker Preparation	Johnson	1977	649 Ex-Offenders	Program Completion Discharged Resumes Mailed Self- and Agency Placement	9 mos. " " "	84% 55% 4,100 52%		N/A N/A N/A *	
14) Worker Preparation	Barnet	1976	202 Ex-Offenders (67 Ex-Offenders)	Recidivism Recidivism Placement	16 mos. 9 mos. "	4% 2% 76%	50% 30% 25%	* * *	

Table 8. (Continued)

	STUDY			METHOD			RESULTS		
Nature	**Authors**	**Dates**	**N of Population**	**Measures**	**Time**	**Treatment**	**Control**	**Diff**
15) Worker Preparation	Williams & Barnet	1979	(20 Candidates)	Crim. Justice Content	3 mos.	247.26	52.00	*
				Career Skills	"	18.44	10.17	*
				IPS (Written)	"	1.82	1.18	*
				IPS (Performance)	"	2.42	1.74	*
				Security	"	3.48 (12.15)	2.14 (9.45)	*
				Report Writing	"	92.65	48.29	*
			40 Candidates	Physical Fitness	"	14.71	13.14	N.S.
				Program Completion	"	90%		N/A
				Field Placement	"	92%		N/A
				Place Completion	"	91%		N/A
				Job Placement	"	92%		N/A
16) Worker Preparation	Carkhuff	1982b	100 Unemployed	Employment	13 yrs.	80%	25%	*

Table 8. (Continued)

The Effects of the Direct Training of Recipients

STUDY				METHOD		RESULTS		
Nature	Authors	Dates	N of Population	Measures	Time	Treatment	Control	Diff
17) Worker Preparation	Carkhuff & Friel	1974	19 Government Executives	**Interpersonal Skills** Discrimination Communication Problem Solving Program Devel. Consulting & Plan. Applications/Skill Appropriate Uses	8 mos. " " " " " "	.77 2.68 4.21 3.42 3.58 20.00 50%	1.34 1.61 1.42 1.63 1.70 2.00 25%	* * * * * * *
18) Worker Preparation	Vitalo	1981	5 Clinical Staff	Job Performance (Assessment Completion)	3 mos.	37.8%	15%	*
19) Worker Performance	Santantonio, Brown & Cohen	1976	11 Child Care Workers	Observed Communication	1 mo.	2.40	1.68	*
20) Worker Performance	Bierman, Santilli & Carkhuff	1972	84 Head Start Workers	IPS Work Effectiveness Work Change	1 week " "	2.60 96% 88%	1.30 73% 64%	* * *

Table 8. (Continued)

STUDY			METHOD			RESULTS		
Nature	Authors	Dates	N of Population	Measures	Time	Treatment	Control	Diff
21) Worker Preparation	Rocha	1982a	3,000 Directors, Supervisors, Teachers, and Counselors	Staff Integration School Crisis Teacher Transfer School Meetings Community Relations Decision Making	1 year " " " "			* * * * * *
22) Worker Preparation	Chingo	1978	37 Ex-Offenders (24 Ex-Offenders) (35 Ex-Offenders)	Recidivism Total Arrests Employment Job Income	6 mos. " " "	21% +101% 67% $73,331	40% −11% 0 −$11,756	* * * *
23) Worker Performance	Mullins, Quirke & Chapados	1980	23 Service Employees	Goal Attainment	6 mos.	56.90 76th perc. 90%	21.70 32nd perc. 10%	* *
24) Worker Performance	Bushee & Chapados	1980	45 Managers	Opportunity/ Initiating	6 mos.	10:7	10:2	*

Table 8. (Continued)

| STUDY | | | | METHOD | | | RESULTS | | |
Nature	Authors	Dates	N of Population	Measures	Time	Treatment	Control	Diff
25) Organization Productivity	Banks, Cannon, et al.	1983	100 Government Employees	Work Quantity	1 year	+ 7%		*
				Work Quality	"	+ 9%		*
				Process Movement	"	+ 2.75 levels		*
				IPS Skill Acquisition	"	+ 1.3 levels		*
				IPS Skill Applications				
				Work Plans	"	89% positive		*
				Task Identification	"	74% positive		*
				Reporting Proced.	"	77% positive		*
				Info. Applications	"	75% positive		*
				Indiv. Task Measures				
				Work Plan Usage (Weekly)	"	69%		*
				Work Plan Usage (Monthly)	"	90%		*
				Work Plan Value	"	82%		*
				Reporting Proced. (Monthly)	"	95%		*
				Reporting Proced. Value	"	85%		*

Table 8. (Concluded)

STUDY			METHOD			RESULTS		
Nature	Authors	Dates	N of Population	Measures	Time	Treatment	Control	Diff
25) Organization Productivity (Concluded)				**Agency Task Meas.** Role Clarification Work Coordination Work Planning Work Producing Crisis Reduction Commun. Improve. Assignment Clarification	= = = = = = =	60% 65% 90% 70% 40% 70% 75%		* * * * * * *
26) Organization Productivity	Kelly	1983	14 Word Processors 44 Word Proc.	Number of Problems Confidence in Skills	½–1 ½ yrs. Immed.	2.57 1.00	4.14 3.85–4.57	* *
27) Organization Productivity	Carkhuff	1983b	13 Business Employees	$ Output Personnel Input Individual Performance Profit	1 year " " "	+ 25% − 16% + 48% + 50%		* * * * * *

revisions. Tyler (1972) established the additional effects of reducing students' feelings of inadequacy and confusion with regard to careers while Friel and his associates (1974) produced significant improvements in career maturity and parental involvement. Inman and Harberts (1976) established similar skill improvements based upon a vocational cluster approach to training. Danley (1980), in turn, found significant improvements in job-seeking and placement at a relatively small cost per youth ($51.45). Jeter and her associates (1975) found that 75% of the students with IPS-based career skills training were selected for employment (for a variety of IPS-based reasons) while only nine percent of those in the control group were selected. Lumley (1976) demonstrated differences on a variety of indices of self-concept and self-realization of manpower students.

Holder, Friel, and their associates explored the basic components of a comprehensive IPS-based career skills training program: work experience, career development skills, and employability skills training. In terms of work experience, they found that 100% of the youth involved were able to place themselves in a work experience, 42% with jobs related to their career goals, and 7% earning incentive pay (Holder and Friel, 1972). In terms of the skill areas, they established an increase in quantity and quality of career skills (Holder, Friel and Tyler, 1979), employability (Holder and Mallory, 1979, in Holder, 1982), and vocational skills (Friel, Holder and Mallory, 1979). Finally, while minimizing dropouts from the program, 95.8% of the students were able to place themselves versus 65% to 83% of the control students (Friel, Franckowiak and Holder, 1979). These studies are illustrations of straightforward technological programs designed to achieve highly operational human goals.

Working with ex-offenders on adult employment, several dramatic sets of results were established. Johnson (1977) found that ex-offenders could be trained in IPS-based self-placement skills that double their rate of placement. Barnet (1976) found very low recidivism rates accompanying very high placement rates. It may be hypothesized that people who are gainfully employed are less likely to repeat offenses.

In related studies, Williams and Barnet (1979) designed an IPS-based criminal justice employment program. Teaching the criminal justice content along with career, IPS, security, report writing, and physical fitness, they achieved the following results: 90% completed the program; of those, 92% were placed in the field; of those, 91%

completed field placement; of those, 92% were placed on a job. Similarly, Carkhuff, Griffin, and Berenson (Carkhuff, 1971b) designed an operational career development and placement program for unemployed people. Making IPS a critical dimension of all work activities involving other humans, they implemented systematic training and internship experiences to place the people on jobs. Now, a thirteen-year follow-up reveals that 80% of those people continue to be employed gainfully in positions ranging from social casework technicians through industry and government executives, including one state senator (Carkhuff, 1982a). It is noteworthy that informal follow-up programs were part of the total design. Again, IPS-based training moving programmatically toward highly operational human goals is the preferred mode of intervening.

In one of the earliest IPS-based studies of work performance, Carkhuff and Friel (1974 in Carkhuff, 1983b) provided state government officials with skills training in IPS, decision making and problem solving, program and systems development, and consulting and planning. They demonstrated significant differences on these and related real-life indices; the applications per skill area improved 1,000%; the appropriate uses of the skills improved 100%.

A number of studies of worker performance related IPS training to improved productivity. Vitalo (1981) improved the job performance of clinical staff by increasing their assessment of not only IPS but work effectiveness and work change indices of Head Start teachers. Bierman, Santilli, and Carkhuff (1972) demonstrated significant effects in not only IPS but also work effectiveness and change of Head Start workers. Santanton, Brown, and Cohen (1976) improved the observed levels of communication of childcare workers. Rocha (1982c) demonstrated the effects of IPS-based training on school staff integration, crises, transfers, meetings, community relations, and decision making. Chingo (1978), working with ex-offenders, demonstrated not only a significant reduction in recidivism and total arrests, but also a significant improvement in employment and job income.

In further extensions of worker performance improvement, Mullins, Quirke, and Chapados (1980) demonstrated more than 250% greater goal attainment and 900% more direct service for IPS-trained employees than employees in an almost identical control condition. Similarly, IPS-trained managers demonstrated a significantly higher level of initiative than untrained managers (Bushee and Chapados, 1980).

In studies of agency productivity, Banks and his associates (1983) designed and implemented an IPS-based management-by-communication system. Training an entire government agency from clerical help through policy-makers, they established a 7% improvement in work quantity and a 9% improvement in work quality. Again, communication is a central ingredient in any cohesively working agency.

Kelly (1983) addressed the perennial problem of word processing. Assuming that secretaries made approximately 20% to 40% of the potential processing applications, he intervened to offer IPS-based word processing skills training. He found significant differences in favor of the trained group in confidence improvement in word processing task performance and problems encountered.

Carkhuff (1983b) demonstrated the effects of systematic intervention programs. Training industry staff in IPS and processing skills to improve individual performance and planning skills to improve agency productivity, he obtained the following results: +25% dollar output; −16% personnel input; +48% individual performance; +50% profit. It is important to emphasize that both follow-up and environmental support systems were installed.

In summary, the benefits of the direct training of workers are demonstrated. In all 27 studies (100%) and 115 of 117 indices (98%) the results are positive.

Again, systematic training of workers in IPS along with other skills appeared to be a critical source of effect in individual employment and worker productivity. In particular, the worker productivity projects of Carkhuff emphasized formal and informal follow-ups and environmental support programs.

8 | Summary and Overview

The reported effects of the interpersonal functioning of helpers and the direct IPS-based training of helpees may be seen most clearly in Table 9. Table 9 summarizes the results for the studies and indices of helpee living, learning, and working outcomes. As can be seen, there are a total of 164 studies assessing a total of 784 indices. One hundred thirty-one (131) of the studies had exclusively positive results while 27 more had predominantly positive results. Seven hundred eighteen (718) of the 784 indices assessed yielded positive results.

These effects are summarized in a more succinct form in Table 10. As can be seen, by far the great majority of studies and indices assessed yielded positive results. Overall, 96% of the studies are exclusively or predominantly positive; 92% of the indices are positive.

Summary

There are several sets of summary propositions that we may draw from these results:

1. **The effects of helper interpersonal functioning upon recipient outcomes are positive and significant.**
   A summary of the effects of helpers upon helpee outcome indices suggests that interpersonal skills are a core ingredient in any HRD effort. Ninety-six percent (96%) of the studies and 92% of the indices yield positive outcomes. Clearly, these helper effects hold across living, learning, and working outcomes.

2. **IPS training is the source of high levels of helper interpersonal functioning.**
   In all but ten instances, systematic IPS training was the source of helper interpersonal functioning. Thus, in 85% of the studies, IPS training was directly related to the effects of helping. That is to say, alone or in combination with other skills, IPS training is a significant source of effect in helping efforts.

3. **The effects of direct IPS training of recipients upon helpee outcomes are positive and significant.**

   The direct IPS training of recipients is a significant source of recipient outcome benefits. In 96% of the studies and 92% of the indices, the reported results were positive. Thus, alone or in combination with other skills, direct IPS training of recipients is a potential preferred mode of treatment.

4. **Positive results are describable and predictable while negative results are statistical exceptions.**

   Ninety-six percent (96%) of the studies and 92% of the indices had positive outcomes. Thus, putting the issues of rater level of functioning (Cannon and Carkhuff, 1969) and minimal level of helper functioning (Berenson and Mitchell, 1974; Carkhuff, 1969; Carkhuff and Berenson, 1976) aside, it may be concluded that negative result studies and indices tend toward being statistical or random exceptions (i.e., alpha (α) at the .05 to .10 levels).

5. **Positive IPS outcomes are a consequence of systematic efforts while negative results are design exceptions.**

   Systematically derived results involve systematic design: systematic training design, systematic treatment design, systematic follow-up and systematic environmental support. When present, these ingredients of systematic designs will yield systematic outcomes. When any one of these ingredients is absent, there is an increasing prospect for non-significant or even negative results. Thus, for example, without systematic training, variability in interpersonal functioning will be restricted and the relationships with various outcome indices become problematic.

Processing Skills

In this context, it is extremely important to emphasize IPS as processing skills, alone or in combination with other processing skills. In many of the studies, IPS are employed as the single intervention: the interveners are trained in IPS to intervene with the recipients, or the recipients are trained directly in IPS.

Where IPS are employed as the sole intervention, they are nevertheless processing skills. Because of the nature of the skills, the stimuli are processed into responses rather than conditioned to responses.

Table 9. A Summary Index of Results of IPS Studies and Indices of Helpee Living, Learning, and Working Outcomes

SOURCES OF EFFECT

OUTCOMES (HELPERS)	HELPERS: Exclusively Positive Results (+ +)	Predominantly Positive Results (+ +/-)	Non-Significant or Mixed Results (+/-)	Predominantly Negative Results (- +/-)	Exclusively Negative Results (-)	HELPEES: Exclusively Positive Results (+ +)	Predominantly Positive Results (+ +/-)	Non-Significant or Mixed Results (+/-)	Predominantly Negative Results (- +/-)	Exclusively Negative Results (-)	OUTCOMES (HELPEES)
LIVING (Table 2) Studies (N = 22)	14	6	2			25	7	2	1		LIVING (Table 6) Studies (N = 36)
LIVING Indices (N = 117)	97		17		3	105		16		4	LIVING Indices (N = 129)
LEARNING (Tables 3 & 4) Studies (N = 32)	22	9	1			25	1				LEARNING (Table 7) Studies (N = 26)
LEARNING Indices (N = 280)	241		19		1	78		1			LEARNING Indices (N = 79)
WORKING (Table 5) Studies (N = 22)	19	3				25	2	2			WORKING (Table 8) Studies (N = 27)
WORKING Indices (N = 88)	83		3			115					WORKING Indices (N = 117)

105

Table 9. (Concluded)

SOURCES OF EFFECT

HELPERS

OUTCOMES SUBTOTAL	Exclusively Positive Results (0-+)	Predominantly Positive Results (+ +/-)	Non-Significant or Mixed Results (0+/-)	Predominantly Negative Results (-/+0)	Exclusively Negative Results (-)
Studies (N = 76)	55	18	3		
Indices (N = 464)	421		39		4

HELPEES

OUTCOMES SUBTOTAL	Exclusively Positive Results (0-+)	Predominantly Positive Results (+ +/-)	Non-Significant or Mixed Results (0+/-)	Predominantly Negative Results (-/+0)	Exclusively Negative Results (-)
Studies (N = 88)	75	10	2	1	
Indices (N = 324)	301		19		4

GRAND TOTAL

	Exclusively Positive Results (0-+)	Predominantly Positive Results (+ +/-)	Non-Significant or Mixed Results (0+/-)	Predominantly Negative Results (-/+0)	Exclusively Negative Results (-)
Studies (N = 164)	130	28	5	1	
Indices (N = 780)	722		58		8

Table 10. A Summary Index of Percentages of Predominantly Positive Results of IPS Studies and Indices of Helpee Living, Learning, and Working Outcomes

OUTCOME	HELPERS	HELPEES	OUTCOMES
LIVING (Table 2)			*LIVING* (Table 6)
Studies (N = 22)	91% Positive	91% Positive	Studies (N = 35)
Indices (N = 117)	83% Positive	84% Positive	Indices (N = 128
LEARNING (Tables 3 & 4)			*LEARNING* (Table 7)
Studies (N = 32)	97% Positive	100% Positive	Studies (N = 26)
Indices (N = 261)	92% Positive	99% Positive	Indices (N = 78)
WORKING (Table 5)			*WORKING* (Table 8)
Studies (N = 22)	100% Positive	100% Positive	Studies (N = 27)
Indices (N = 83)	96% Positive	98% Positive	Indices (N = 117)
SUBTOTAL			**SUBTOTAL**
Studies (N = 76)	96% Positive	96% Positive	Studies (N = 88)
Indices (N = 461)	92% Positive	92% Positive	Indices (N = 323)
GRAND TOTAL			
Studies (N = 164)	96% Positive		
Indices (N = 784)	92% Positive		

In other typical interpersonal programs, helpers are conditioned to make specific responses to specific stimuli. The critical processing phase in IPS occurs after the content, affect, and meaning are responded to by the intervener (Carkhuff, 1983a). It is at this point that the intervener personalizes the meaning, problems, or deficits, and goals of the recipients. Thus, the intervener produces responses that go beyond the stimuli presented by the recipients by personalizing the processing. When the recipients are trained directly to make personalized responses to the meaning, problems, and goals of themselves or others, they also involve themselves in interpersonal processing.

In some studies, IPS are employed in conjunction with problem-solving skills and program-development skills (Carkhuff, 1969, 1973, 1974, 1975). Thus, in the living skills areas, the work of Chapados and Vitalo and their associates incorporated these complementary processing skills in training helpers for interventions or training helpees directly as the preferred mode of treatment. In these instances, the helpers and recipients had the additional processing benefits of being able to programmatically select preferred courses of action to solve their problems or achieve their goals.

In the learning areas, Aspy and his associates employ cognitive functioning strategies in conjunction with the IPS. Thus, Aspy's teachers were trained in the skills of analyzing situations and solving problems as well as in memorizing facts, concepts, and principles. In the direct training of learners, Berenson and his associates taught the learners specific learning-to-learn processing skills in conjunction with IPS-processing. Thus, the learners were taught specific learning strategies with which to process reading and math content: exploring where they are in relation to the learning experience; understanding where they want or need to be; and acting to get from where they are to where they want or need to be.

In the working skills areas, Pierce and his associates designed the "Get–Give–Merge and Go" program to emphasize "Problem–Reason–Direction" processing. Thus, the four-step IPS-based communication process guides the managers and supervisors through the three-step performance improvement process identifying and solving specific performance problems. In the direct training of employees, Carkhuff and his associates taught specific productivity processing strategies with dramatically positive results. Basically, productivity processing involves exploring, understanding, and acting to accomplish the productivity goals of increasing results outputs while reducing resource inputs (Carkhuff, 1983b).

In this regard, Carkhuff (1983b) sees productive individuals as possessing three critical ingredients: 1) productivity values to which they dedicate their other ingredients; 2) processing skills which transform the stimuli into productive responses; and 3) interpersonal skills which serve to relate individuals with individuals and organizations, and to disseminate new learnings concerning improving performance.

Similarly, Carkhuff (1983b) sees productive organizations as processing four critical sets of ingredients: 1) maximum responsiveness to information input; 2) maximum human and mechanical processing of the input; 3) maximum initiation of new services and products as outputs, with information by-products; and 4) maximum and constant monitoring of individual performance and organizational productivity.

Clearly, the key ingredients to productive individuals and organizations are productivity processing and interpersonal processing (Carkhuff, 1983b). The productivity processing serves to analyze, operationalize, and technologize the components, functions, and processes of the content, materials or experience. The interpersonal processing serves to share interdependently as teachers and learners reap the benefits of that processing. The more programmatically the productivity processing and interpersonal processing skills are taught and implemented, the more incremental will be our performances as individuals and our productivity as organizations.

Intervention Issues

In this context, let us describe in further detail the activities or stations of a systematic intervention design whether focusing on treatment or training (Carkhuff, 1983b). The intervention design is implemented in the following seven activities: 1) determining the human productivity goals you wish to accomplish; 2) assessing the context in order to determine its task requirements of people to meet the goals; 3) specifying the skill objectives that comprise the task requirements; 4) developing the skill steps and supportive knowledge content to achieve the skill objectives; 5) developing the delivery plan to deliver the skills content; 6) making the delivery; and 7) receiving the delivery (recipient).

In reverse order, we find the five levels of outcome assessments: 1) assessing the interaction between trainer or helper and recipients in facilitating the recipients' skill acquisition (process); 2) assessing the recipients' acquisition of the skill content (acquisition); 3) assessing the recipients' application of the skills in a simulated real-life experience (application); 4) assessing the recipients' transfer of skills to functioning in the real-life context (transfer); and 5) assessing the costs and benefits of the recipients' real-life functioning (productivity) (Carkhuff, 1983b).

These seven stations of implementation and five stations of assessment comprise the 12 stations of systematic intervention in any area. They are recycled within and between consulting, training, installing, or treating, follow-up and environmental support systems. They comprise the comprehensive intervention systems design for any human outcome (Carkhuff, 1983b).

Several issues of intervention remain. Not the least of these is the issue of recipient contribution to variance. There is a growing contention that the client is the primary source of variance in helping (Lambert, 1982) and that the learner is the primary source of variance in learning (Gage, 1977). Again, we acknowledge that the recipients contribute to intervention effectiveness. However, we find the prospect of recipient dominance frightening and without prospects for movement and, above all, change or growth. We continue to suggest strongly, based upon extensive evidence, that the contribution of recipients is dominant with low-level helpers and minimal with high-level helpers (Carkhuff, 1969, 1971; Carkhuff and Berenson, 1976). The recipient is, after all, defined by his or her skill deficit. There is now extensive empirical evidence to support the proposition that when untrained helpers are themselves deficient of systems designs and technologies for consulting, training, treatment, follow-up, and environmental support, the recipients dominate the sources of effectiveness in helping (Carkhuff, 1982b): recipients maintain their same skill-less behaviors in interaction with skill-less helpers. Recipients acquire skills and become productive in interaction with skillful helpers. Indeed, it is the very essence of helping that the helpees, themselves, become helpers.

In this context, in our own work, we have conceived of our task as discovering high-level functioning or exemplary helpers. The remaining tasks are direct and straightforward: to systematically analyze the dimensions of the high-functioning helper; to systematically operationalize the dimensions of the high-functioning helper; to systematically technologize the programs for achieving these operational goals; and to systematically transmit these technological skills to others. In short, our task was to study and evaluate "winners" and transform "losers" into "winners". It was not our purpose to randomly select and replicate the effects of "losers".

The issue of the differential effects of helper IPS and direct training of recipient IPS is an interesting one. Collingwood (1976, 1978) concludes from his own research that perhaps 50% of the variance is people and the other 50% is programs. He reported finding recidivism rates that stabilized at around 10% when he had a talented and well-trained staff. When the top half of the staff talent was replaced, he found that the recidivism rate stabilized at around 20% against a base rate of approximately 60% recidivism. He suggested that the helping programs had become greater sources of effect. Our own estimates from previous work (Carkhuff and Berenson, 1976) apportion 50% of effect to people, 40% to programs, and the remaining 10% to environmental support, depending upon the people and program variables.

The issue that any training may organize and systematize any helping endeavor remains. To be sure, any program that moves systematically toward its goals is more effective than any program that does not. In this context, the IPS training program is one that moves programmatically toward attaining human goals. While the designs, controls, and analyses vary, the results are robust and consistent across studies. Phenomena that emerge only under carefully controlled conditions and analyses are often of questionable human value. Whether other interpersonal programs can do as well or better in impacting human beings remains an empirical question. What is established is that IPS programs do produce human results. No other HRD program has been so extensively implemented and so thoroughly researched.

Additional issues of testing and the significance of results converge. Earlier pilot studies evidenced more mixed results than later ones as the authors, including our own work, used a variety of test indices to assess outcomes. Succinctly, we learned that we obtained those outcomes for which we trained or treated the populations. Additional generalization results were purely serendipitous and, indeed, led to new research and demonstration. These early studies were done largely to effect living outcomes; thus, their slightly lower level of positive results. Later demonstrations defined their goals more operationally and behaviorally. Clearly, the more concretely we define our goals, the more likely we are to achieve our outcome. Other forms of assessing outcomes, including traditional objective and projective testing, become irrelevant. Such assessments were historically a product of the principle of research that attempted to keep outcome indices independent of the intervention program. We can now assess the impact of systematic interventions on indices of real-life functioning and productivity. We no longer need theoretical constructs of reality because we can now test reality directly. Most important, we can develop our new indices on the basis of reality-based ideals which incorporate certain critical interpersonal dimensions.

In summary, the most important issue is the critical nature of interpersonal skills. They serve to enable people to assume the frames of reference of others. They facilitate: the exploration of where others are in relation to a particular experience; the understanding of where others want or need to be; and the action behavior to get from where they are to where they want to be. In this regard, IPS are critical ingredients in the implementation of any programs involving human beings, whether individual, small-group, or large-group treatment or training. They may be used in conjunction with any other skills to accomplish any intervention goals involving humans in living, learning, and working performance (Carkhuff, 1983b).

9 Conclusions and Implications

The implications for parenting and helping, teaching and training, employing and working are profound. When helpers or supervisors are trained to relate effectively to all levels within an organization—up and sideways as well as down—then they and their recipients are productive in achieving mutually beneficial goals. Further, when the recipients are trained directly in relating effectively—up, down, and sideways—then they are productive in achieving their goals.

Relatedly, we insure the success of our endeavors by meeting the following conditions in our systems interventions: 1) the consultant-trainers are functioning at high levels of interpersonal skills which enable them to expand the frames of reference of the decision-makers; 2) the program implementers are trained to function at high levels of interpersonal skills; 3) the program implementers use their interpersonal skills to process input and feedback from the recipients upon installation; 4) the consultant-trainers and program implementers use their interpersonal skills to conduct follow-up programs to insure the ongoing success of the program; and 5) the consultant-trainers and program implementers converge to create a supportive environment for the program.

In this context, comprehensive intervention designs have been introduced in the living, learning, and working skills arenas. These studies have already had a tremendous impact on the helping and teaching professions as well as growing impact upon policy-makers, managers, and supervisors in the private and public sectors.

Living

Within the helping professions, Anthony (1982) points out the great difference in the use of the words "skills" in general or "helping skills" in particular in the literature. Using the 1974 American Personnel and Guidance Association Keynote Address (Carkhuff, 1974) as the milestone, Anthony found the mention of helping skills' before the address to be almost exclusively by Carkhuff and his colleagues. Subsequent to the address, the use of "helping skills" is almost universal. Even the use of "helper" and "helpee" was stimulated by skills-based approaches to helping.

In addition, entire counseling movements have culminated in IPS-based practices. The lay counseling movement initiated in the 1960's (Carkhuff and Truax, 1965a, 1965b) has been operationalized in "functional professionalism" as distinguished from credentialed professionalism. Hospital attendants, ministers, community helpers, and the like with IPS-skills-based training are accepted as potential helpers.

Historically, centers of treatment activity employing both lay and professional helpers have included the following: the community-based efforts of Chapados and his associates in Minnesota; the community mental health work of Cohen, Cohen and Vitalo in Ohio; the medical counseling work of Gazda and his colleagues in Georgia; the therapeutic efforts of Egan and others in Illinois; and the consultative efforts of Cash and associates in California.

Led by Anthony and his associates (Anthony, 1979, 1980), the psychiatric rehabilitation movement has assumed leadership in the training of thousands of professional and lay helpers in the following areas: diagnostic planning (Anthony, Pierce and Cohen, 1979a), rehabilitation programming (Anthony, Pierce and Cohen, 1979), community service support (Cohen, Vitalo, Anthony and Pierce, 1979), instruction (Anthony, Cohen and Pierce, 1979) and professional evaluation (Cohen, Anthony, Pierce and Spaniol, 1979).

Some movements like the correctional counseling movement have institutionalized IPS-based training for all staff. The correctional counseling movement was originated in 1969 when inner-city community personnel trained the first wave of 30 federal and state line supervisors in Springfield, Massachusetts (Carkhuff, 1971a; Hall, 1970). The next year, the graduates conducted their own training programs under the guidance of the original staff (Hall, 1971a). The third year, two representatives from every federal institution were trained in Dallas, Texas (Hall, 1971b). These representatives returned to their correctional settings and trained their entire staffs involving some 5,700 personnel (Hall, 1972). Today, all federal prison personnel receive two weeks of preservice training, including 40 hours of IPS-based "decency skills" as well as regular refresher courses (Hall, 1973). The Federal Bureau of Prisons can now boast one of the highest levels of human standards of any major organized institution in the world.

Further, "training as treatment" has established itself as perhaps the most revolutionary treatment concept of our times. Instead of working in one-to-one relationships with helpees, thousands of helpers are training groups of helpees in the skills they need to help themselves. The "training as treatment" approach, in the hands of skilled practitioners, is not only more efficient; it is also more effective! Treatment centers such as those engineered by personnel like Anthony, Chapados, Vitalo and their respective associates have demonstrated their efficacy in terms of both human benefits and cost savings (Carkhuff, 1983).

For example, Bierman's models for parent training have been incorporated as models for self-help and community support programs throughout Canada. Basically, parents and concerned citizens are trained in IPS-based skills to, first, help themselves and, second, help others, including especially their children. These programs have demonstrated their cost-effectiveness (Bierman, Davison, Finkelman, Leonidas, Lumley and Simister, 1976) and stand as a potential preferred mode of community treatment and support.

Learning

The learning studies have had a growing impact upon futuristic educational practices. The Aspy IPS teaching models have been based directly upon the Carkhuff IPS models, since Aspy and his associates found the IPS to be most highly related to teacher performance and learner outcomes (Aspy, Aspy and Roebuck, 1982). The Aspy teacher training approaches have been installed in educational systems in all 50 states as well as dozens of foreign countries in Europe, Asia, and South America under the auspices of the National Consortium for Humanizing Education.

It is important to emphasize that these IPS conditions hold in studies of teacher IPS effects upon learners around the world. In this context, Tausch and his associates, while initially questioning the Aspy–Carkhuff results, have gone on to replicate the essential findings with German teacher and pupil populations (Bruh, Schwab and Tausch, 1980; Hoder, Tausch and Weber, 1976; Klyne, 1976; Joost, 1978; Pize-Kettner, Ahrbeck, Scheibel and Tausch, 1978; Rudolph, 1975; Rudolph, Langer and Tausch, 1980; Tausch, Kettner, Steinbach and Tonnies, 1973; Tausch and Tausch, 1980; Tausch, Wittern and Albus, 1976; Theig, Steinbach and Tausch, 1978). Their data, not summarized in this report, is summarized by Aspy and Roebuck (1983).

In addition, lead teachers in every state in the United States have been trained in teaching skills under the auspices of the National and State Education Associations (Banks, 1980; Griffin, 1980). The IPS models have been the basis for the development of the LEAST model of discipline (Carkhuff, Griffin and Mallory, 1978; Mallory, 1979; N.E.A., 1978, 1979) which has been adapted and transmitted to more than 200,000 teachers by the National Education Association. For the reader's purposes, the LEAST acronym represents the following stages of discipline: L—Leave the student behavior alone (if it is not particularly troublesome); E—End the action (if the behavior is troublesome); A—Attend and respond interpersonally upon intervening; S—Spell out the directions for the students' performance; and T—Track the students' progress.

Self-facilitation "teaching as treatment" approaches have begun to blossom. Berenson's approach to preservice education for business and human service personnel in Massachusetts is to teach IPS-based human processing or learning-to-learn skills before teaching anything else (Carkhuff, 1983b). Collingwood is conducting inservice "teaching as treatment" groups in physical and interpersonal areas for teachers in the Dallas, Texas, school system (Collingwood, 1982).

Rocha continues to implement her comprehensive statewide design in Brazil, while setting up special pilot sites to emphasize learner achievement of higher order processing skills. In a comprehensive statewide design, Griffin (1982) is initiating an IPS-based program for thousands of teachers in the Georgia Educational Association. There, he is training the teachers who are, in turn, training learners as well as administrators and parents and other business and community support personnel in all of those skills related to developing an effectively integrated learning delivery system. For the teachers, these skills emphasize content development, lesson planning, teaching delivery skills, and teaching management skills along with interpersonal skills. For the learners, the skills emphasize content analysis, teaching reception, and learning management skills along with learning-to-learn skills. For the administrators, the skills emphasize interpersonal and management skills. For the community support personnel, the skills include interpersonal skills in conjunction with their specialty skills: parent support skills (parents), work support skills (business and government), and community support skills (community-at-large).

In most of these learning skills applications, the projects are maximizing results outputs while minimizing resource inputs. The inputs are primarily training interventions. The model for productivity is the demonstration made by Aspy (Aspy and Roebuck, 1977) where he intervened to give third-grade reading teachers three cards. Each card had one feeling word which the teacher was to use after each recitation by the students. Thus, for example, the teachers said: "You feel *sad* because you did not do well"; "You feel *angry* because you still can't get that word'; or "You feel *happy* because you did so well". The students improved dramatically in their ability to read because the teachers had reinforced them by entering their frames of reference. All learning begins with the learners' frames of reference. These results contrast vividly with third-grade reading practices where, after student recitation, it is most typical for the great majority of teachers to say, "Next!" This simple demonstration is a model of productivity: maximizing achievement while minimizing investment.

Working

In terms of worker preparation, Friel, Holder, and their associates have established human-based and computer-based career achievement skills models in the state of Michigan at the following levels: career development models (Carkhuff and Friel, 1974; Holder, 1982); delivery systems (Battenschlag, 1974; Friel, Drake, Tyler and Mallory, 1972); and technologies that emphasize career awareness, decision making, planning, and placement (Battenschlag, et al., 1974; Friel, 1972; Friel and Holder, 1979; Friel, Holder and Franckowiak, 1979, 1980; Friel, Mallory and Holder, 1980; Holder, 1980; Holder, Friel and Tyler, 1979; Holder and Tyler, 1978). These models have been replicated and extended in many states in the U.S.A.

Perhaps the most recent and significant developments in the working skills area are the applications of the "GGMG–PRD" skills. Based upon the work of Pierce and his associates, the early work by Holder and Schultz (1982) has already culminated in millions of dollars of cost-avoidance savings in the one year follow-up at the Fort Worth Division of General Dynamics. These results have been replicated in other private sector settings: Electronics (Rowe and Shultz, 1982); Convair (Douds, 1983); AMOCO (Feder, 1982a, 1982b); ARCO Alaska (Holder, 1983); Abitibi-Price (Brillinger and Friel, 1981). The results have also been replicated in the public sector by Pierce (1982). Indeed, Pierce found IPS to relate more powerfully to productivity than any other management or supervisory skill.

The managers and supervisors have found the "GGMG–PRD" to be significantly more cost-beneficial in terms of time and dollar investments than the old "Give and Go" style characteristic of authoritarian industry in the Industrial Age. In general, the "Give and Go" style, while initially efficient, precipitated cumulative crises because neither managers nor employees agreed upon the images of the tasks to be performed. Conversely, "GGMG–PRD", while requiring an initial investment of time, proactively precluded the crises in task performance. "GGMG–PRD" does indeed appear to be the preferred mode of relating within and between interdependent organizational networks in the Age of Information.

Similarly, in the direct training of employees, Banks and his associates (1983) found that they could increase organizational productivity significantly by training all employees in IPS and processing skills. Kelly (1983), operating from the IBM "office of the future," found that he could increase word processing performance significantly by teaching IPS and human processing skills such as problem solving and program development in addition to the mechanical, computer processing skills. Finally, Carkhuff (1982a) demonstrated significant increases in individual performance and organizational productivity while reducing resource expenditures by teaching IPS and processing skills. In all of these instances of working skills applications, individual performance and organizational productivity were improved significantly while resource inputs were held constant or reduced.

Organized movements in the working area are less likely than those in the living and learning areas. However, individual industries have attended programmatically to working skills development and outcome. For example, General Dynamics Corporation, one of the world's largest high-tech corporations, has institutionalized IPS-based training for all of its managers and supervisors throughout different divisions (Carkhuff, 1983b). Thousands of managers use their IPS skills in implementing performance appraisal, employee development, work incentive, or any of the other quality assurance programs calculated to improve productivity. In addition, the corporation has attempted to incorporate both follow-up and environmental support programs to maintain both the training and installation effects. Further, the corporation's IPS-based management training programs have had a dramatic influence upon personnel planning and HRD planning in major corporations like those holding membership in the Cowdrick Group. There is a growing recognition in business and industry of the need for interpersonal processing between employees. Also, there is a strong movement toward interdependent organizations in which each employee, at whatever level, processes and shares products based upon his or her own unique data bases.

Again, systematically-organized worker training programs are less likely in industry than in other areas. Perhaps this is because of lingering management attitudes concerning humans as "replaceable machines" rather than as the sources of productivity. For example, often "quality circles" fail to produce desired results because management uses "reduction-in-force" indices of their success. In other words, the workers are supposed to participate in designing their own demise. Yet IPS-based human processing programs loom as the most potent source of improving productivity (Carkhuff, 1983b).

Perhaps the most significant models for the private sector come out of the public sector. Bergeson and her associates in the Women's Caucus of the National Education Association (N.E.A.) have overseen the design and implementation of the IPS-based Women's Leadership Training Program. There, tens of thousands of women teachers learned decision-making skills to take control of their own lives before learning group facilitation and processing skills leading to improved performance (Carkhuff, 1983b). In the other instance, in her capacity as Vice President of the Washington Education Association, Bergeson has trained the entire state educational leadership in IPS, thus establishing a model for facilitative rather than adversarial negotiation (Bergeson, 1983). While these innovations pose potential political problems for private organizations just as they do for the N.E.A., they are models for interdependent relations within and between individuals, units, and industries as well as between management and labor forces. We are all confronted by the productivity challenges of the Information Age—teachers as well as school boards and citizens, labor as well as management and customers. Achieving productivity goals requires human processing and human relating to produce more while expending less.

In summary, IPS are critical human ingredients because they facilitate the accomplishment of human goals. IPS help people to explore each others' frames of reference. IPS help people to understand the objectives for the tasks at hand. Finally, IPS help people to act upon their shared objectives. In short, IPS facilitate the focusing of human efforts.

IPS help us to live more effectively with our families at home and to help more effectively our counselees in our counseling centers. IPS help us to teach and learn more effectively in our schools and training centers. IPS help us to work more effectively at our individual stations and in our organizations at work. In short, IPS facilitate our human productivity.

Overall, we stand about a 95% chance of accomplishing any human purposes when we have introduced interpersonal skills at high levels. Whether we train helpers or teachers or employers or their recipients in IPS, we accomplish our objectives far beyond the probabilities of chance. Conversely, when we do not introduce IPS at high levels, we stand a random chance of succeeding in any human endeavor. In conclusion, human productivity is, in part, a function of people's abilities to process interpersonally. Interpersonally skilled people, understanding one another accurately, can succeed at any reasonable human endeavor.

10 Human Processing and Human Productivity

Sources of Economic Growth

Historically, capital and natural resources accounted for the great majority of growth in productivity. Today, they account for a small minority of productivity growth. For example, in the first part of the century, capital and natural resources, including minerals, energy, and land, accounted for approximately 75% of our gross national product (GNP). Today, they account for less than one-fourth of GNP.

Human and information resources are the great sources of productivity in the Information Age. Since the early 1900s, these resources have become increasingly dominant in relation to capital and natural resources. Improved quality and reconfiguration of labor through education, training, retraining, and "on-the-job know-how" have consistently accounted for the greatest amount of productivity improvement and growth in national income. In general, the higher the quality of human and information resources, the higher the growth in productivity.

When economists project the sources of economic growth, they conceive of factor or resource inputs and productivity components or organizational processing as the dominant sources (Carnavale, 1983). The resource input sources emphasize human and capital resources. The organizational processing sources include information resources or advancements in knowledge and human resources or, in their terms, skilled labor. In turn, the human resources are accounted for primarily by education and training and secondarily by health and workforce composition.

The moderate to high projections in national income range from 3.4% to 4.8% over the 1980–1990 period. The resource inputs account for between 1.8% and 2.2% of this growth. In turn, the organizational processing accounts for from 1.6% to 2.6% of this growth. In general, we may think of the input and processing component contributions as being approximately equal. However, the inputs decrease in contribution and the processing increases in con-tribution as the productivity growth projections increase. In other words, the higher the productivity growth, the greater is the influence of the organizational processing component.

Thus, we may summarize the sources of projected economic growth as in Figure 5. As can be seen, economic growth is accounted for by the resource inputs and organizational processing: the inputs and the processing each account for approximately 50% of the variability in projected economic growth.

$$\text{Economic Growth} = 50\% \text{ Capital Inputs} + 50\% \text{ Organizational Processing}$$

Figure 5. Equation for Economic Growth

When we analyze the resource input components, we find that human capital resources account for the greatest percent of effect. In general, human capital account for around two-thirds or 67% of the input components while other capital resources account for around one-third or 33% of the input components. Other factors, such as natural resources and land, make negligible contributions.

It is important to understand that the human capital inputs to the organization system are outputs of other systems, particularly education and training, but also the home and community. Thus, the human capital inputs bring with them skills, knowledge, and atti-tudes based on previous learning experiences. In other words, the current mode of analyzing resource inputs incorporates information resources within the human capital resources.

Thus, we may represent the equation for resource inputs as in Figure 6. For purposes of calculation, if we allocate the amount of variance ascribed to human capital equally to both human and information resources, we have an approximation of the relative im-pact of these factors: the human, information, and capital resources contribution about equally as resource inputs. It is important to keep in mind that the capital resource inputs, in total, contribute approximately 50% of the variance to overall economic growth. For our purposes, we may say that human, information, and capital resource inputs each contribute in the range of 15%–20% percent of overall economic growth.

Capital Inputs	=	33% Human Capital	+	33% Information Capital	+	33% Other Capital Resources

Figure 6. Equation for Capital Inputs

In turn, the organizational processing component breaks down into human and information capital factors. Advancements in knowledge or "working smarter" account for around half of productivity growth. The quality of labor or personnel accounts for the other half with the effects of some "depressor variables" subtracting from the net effects of knowledge and personnel quality. In addition, there is some tendency for the effects of information capital resources or knowledge to increase as the size of the growth projections increase. In other words, the more efficiently and effectively the personnel work, the greater the growth in productivity.

In short, there is a relationship between human and information capital resources. As the skills of the human capital resources improve, the power of the information capital resources increases. Conversely, as the advancements in knowledge take place, the personnel are empowered. Together, human and information capital resources maintain a synergistic relationship where each contributes to the growth of the other and both contribute to the productivity growth of the organization.

Thus, we may represent the equation for organizational processing as in Figure 7. As can be seen, human and information resources, alone and in interaction ($\leftrightarrow$) with each other, contribute equally to organizational processing. Again, for purposes of calculation, we may say that human and information capital resource processing components each contribute about 25% to overall economic growth.

Organizational Processing (HCD $\leftrightarrow$ ICD)	=	50% Human Capital Development	+	50% Information Capital Development

Figure 7. Equation for Organizational Processing

In summary, we may postulate human and information capital resources as the prepotent sources of effect in economic growth. High quality human and information capital resource inputs account for approximately 30%–35% of overall economic growth. Human and information capital resource processing account for approximately 50% of overall economic growth. Together, human and information capital resources, alone as inputs and processes, and together in synergistic interaction with each other, account for 80%–85% of projected economic growth in the Age of Information.

We may represent an equation for the various sources of economic growth as in Figure 8. As can be seen, the human, information, and other capital resources contribute equally to the 50% of economic growth attributed to resource inputs. In addition, human and information capital resources, alone and in interaction with each other, account for the 50% of economic growth attributed to organizational processing. Again, we should remember that the greater the economic growth, the more potent a contributor is organizational processing (HCD ↔ ICD). Indeed, we may conjecture that the more robust the organizational processing the greater the economic growth.

Economic Growth	=	50% Human and Information Capital Inputs	+	50% Organizational Processing
		17% Human Capital + 17% Information Capital = 17% Other Capital Resources		25% Human Capital + 25% Information Capital

Figure 8. Equation for Sources of Economic Growth

Sources of Human and Information Capital Development

It is important to understand not only the ingredients of economic growth, but also the sources of these ingredients. We must attempt to answer the critical questions: What are the sources of the human and information capital variables that account for 80%–85% of projected economic growth? How can we impact human and information capital resource development to facilitate their contributions to economic growth? In other words, we may posit that individual and interpersonal processing account about equally for human and information resource development. It simply makes good sense that people process, first, independently and then, simultaneously, while processing interpersonally or interdependently with others.

From our own research, we have found interpersonal and individual skills each accounting for approximately 50% of the variability in the human and information processing (HCD $\leftrightarrow$ ICD) which defines organizational processing. We may represent our equation for human capital development as in Figure 9. As can be seen, individual and interpersonal processing contribute about equally to the synergistic interaction of human and information capital development in organizational processing.

Organizational Processing (HCD $\leftrightarrow$ ICD)	=	50% Individual Processing	+	50% Interpersonal Processing

Figure 9. Equation for Human Processing

In addition, we may explore the relationship of education and training to human and information capital development. First, we may attribute the variability of human resource inputs to previous educational experiences in the home and in school. Second, we may explore data from the projections of the economists for the human and information capital development that occurs within the organizational processing component.

We may represent the equation for human capital development within the organizational processing components as in Figure 10. As can be seen, education and training account for approximately 80% of human capital development, while health and workforce composition each account for approximately 10%. For our purposes, of the overall economic growth, education and training accounts for the great majority of the effects of human capital development within the organizational processing component.

Human	=	80%	+	10%	+	10%
Capital		Education		Health		Workforce
Development		and Training				Composition

Figure 10. Equation for Human Capital Development

Thus, between human and information capital inputs and processing, we may conclude that education and training account for more than 50% of human and information capital development: 35% human and information capital inputs; and nearly all of the 25% of human capital development within the organizational processing component.

Finally, we may draw upon our research in other areas of human relations to understand the sources of training effectiveness. We have found that the most critical variables emphasize the trainer's level of functioning in the skills area being taught. Thus, the productive trainer is not only able to teach didactically but, most important, to model representatively the skills being taught. The remaining variance may be attributed to the development and organization of the content and the management of the learners' experiential exercising of the skills.

We may treat education and training in much the same manner as organizational productivity growth. In the instance of training, the training outputs focus on the gain in trainee acquisition, application, and transfer of responses. Thus, training emphasizes transforming naïve human resources into developed or skilled human capital.

We may represent an equation for the effects of training as in Figure 11. As can be seen, the critical sources of training are the training resource inputs and the training process itself. Our own research on the effects of training supports the trainers and trainees along with the content they are processing as the critical sources of effect—in the 80%–85% range—in training gains. In this context, there is evidence to suggest that the prepotent source of effect is the discrepancy between the trainer's and the trainee's initial levels of functioning in the substantive area. In general, the trainees gain about one-half of the discrepancy between their levels of functioning and those of the trainers.

Training Gains = 50% Resource Inputs + 50% Organizational Processing

| 17% Trainer and Trainee Skills + 17% Content Inputs = 17% Capital Equipment | | 5% Trainer and Trainee Processing + 25% Content Processing |

Figure 11. Equation for Effects of Training

Toward Human Processing and Human Productivity

What do these equations for human and information capital development as the sources of economic growth sum to? We may view the critical variables from a different perspective (see Figure 12). As can be seen, education and training accounts for most of individual and interpersonal processing which, in turn, accounts for the vast majority of the human and information capital development variables. In turn, human and information capital variables, alone and in synergistic interaction, account for nearly all of economic productivity. In short, there is nearly a direct-line progression from education to economic growth.

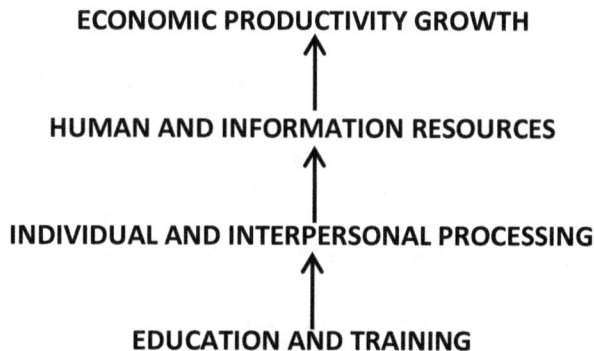

ECONOMIC PRODUCTIVITY GROWTH

↑

HUMAN AND INFORMATION RESOURCES

↑

INDIVIDUAL AND INTERPERSONAL PROCESSING

↑

EDUCATION AND TRAINING

Figure 12. Sources of Human Processing

We may place the sources of human productivity in a still larger perspective (see Figure 13). The interaction of education and the home may be seen as the source of individual and interpersonal processing skills (IPS$_1$ ↔ IPS$_2$) which account for human and information capital development (HCD ↔ ICD). In turn, human and information capital development are the primary sources of economic productivity growth and, it is conjectured, human freedom. Together, economic productivity and freedom are the primary sources of peace and prosperity in our "global village."

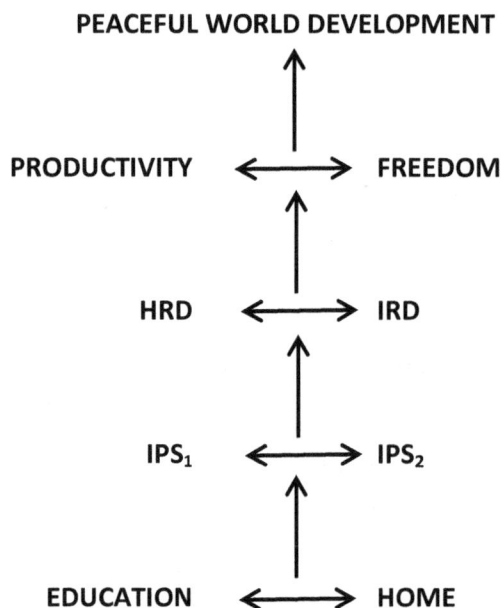

PEACEFUL WORLD DEVELOPMENT

PRODUCTIVITY ⟷ FREEDOM

HRD ⟷ IRD

IPS$_1$ ⟷ IPS$_2$

EDUCATION ⟷ HOME

Figure 13. Sources of Human Productivity

As citizens of an increasingly smaller world, we may conjecture about the relationships of economic productivity and social and political freedom. The relationships may be reasoned logically by observing the differential in productivity in the free and totalitarian systems in the world. A few people simply cannot do the processing required of the many. In short, a free people are a productive people and vice versa.

This is not an ideological but rather a data-based debate. The economic theories of capitalism, communism, and indeed, most modern economic theories are, at best, irrelevant to today's human-

and information-based economies. In this context, it is important to respect—not revere—the past. Ninety-nine percent of the ideation in the history of humankind is occurring right now! It is absurd to follow theorists who—however brilliant—had less than 1% of the data that is currently available.

Instead of traditional economic conditions, we can envision a succession of volcanic-like eruptions of scientific breakthroughs and innovative technologies, thus creating entirely new sources of economic growth. The entrepreneurial and intrepreneurial explosions that follow cannot be accounted for by traditional theories that account for less and less of the variance in economic growth.

The relationship between economic growth and employment growth is also a changing relationship. The expanding employment opportunities generated by the entrepreneurial organizations contrasts vividly with the declining opportunities provided by large, established corporations. Transitionally, such relationships, typified by "Okun's law," are critical to healthy societies: unemployment declines as the economy expands beyond projected growth rates. However, with the extraordinary leverage of human processing, we must anticipate a time when economic productivity is so enormous that unemployment will not be of concern. Indeed, ultimately, we may envision the day when leisure will be the human mode and work may be a unique outlet for those seeking human fulfillment.

The precondition for this growth is human processing. The critical variables emphasize productive processing skills in interaction with the freedom to create. In this context, free enterprise in a free marketplace for organizations and nations is analogous to free choice for individuals.

The hope for prosperity and peace through productive world development lies in increasing both the freedom to create and the productivity to support this freedom: to make the pie large enough to enable the disenfranchised peoples of the world to themselves become free and productive for their own purposes. All of this revolves around an evolving concept of human productivity. Economic productivity involves not only reducing resource investments while increasing results benefits. It emphasizes consumer productivity. Not only do we deliver products and services to consumers. We also deliver benefits. The core benefit is to help the consumers to become more productive at whatever it is they are about. Whether we are parents or teachers, business persons, government officials, or community leaders, our business is to help our consumers stay in business. Consumer productivity is the guiding ethic of all human processing and, indeed, human endeavors.

At the other end of a human productivity delivery system, we must view the parenting—home, family, and community—which provides the human resources that are inputs to education. Currently, the home and family backgrounds account for most of the variance in the human resources exiting the secondary school systems in our country. In other words, learner pre-instructional variables relate very highly with learner post-instructional variables. However, when school personnel interact intensely with home, family, and community components, schools can elevate their ability to account for as much as 50% of the variability in learner resource development.

In summary, when each component of a human productivity delivery system brings itself into intimate and intense relations with the other components, then a systems synergy can produce exponentially more than the sum of the contributions of its components. Each part can impact every other part productively. Each healthy player can contribute more than his or her share through productive human processing. This human processing is the great source of human productivity. Indeed, this is the potentially infinite source of finite human productivity leading to a productive, free, and peaceful world.

Toward Personal Growth

The pursuit of science is at once grand and ennobling, yet highly problematic and humbling. It is an attempt to explicate the unknown—to make the unknown knowable. It is pursued through a mixture of data and research, of interpretation and meaning. Above all, its source is human experience, its gaps are filled by human intuition and are bridged by human conjecture.

There are no longer any laws of science—there never were! There are merely probabilities that serve to guide us to better or more productive probability statements. These formulas for probabilities are pursued by people who are in part disinterested scholars and in part committed artists.

Even Einstein summarized blackboards and books full of data in an artistic equation for communicating a profound yet commercial formula for energy potential: $E = mc^2$. In a similar manner, all scientists—in fact, all people in the Age of Information, for all people are processors—must analyze, synthesize, and operationally define, and then creatively communicate productive information.

All people—like scientists—must live their lives, learn their substance, work their jobs, fulfill their potential just as they test human experience: as tentative hypotheses to be supported or qualified or rejected according to the results of their testing, not in research, but in their momentary experience.

All people—like scientists—must be prepared to change their hypotheses and, thus, their lives with the results of their testing, for the Age of Information is, indeed, just that: an era of enormous information flow that comes to us from all points of our universes—internal as well as external—and at all times in our experience—sleeping as well as waking—human as well as extra-human.

In previous eras, people coined the expression, "the Man." There was, indeed, "the Man." He led the tribes of hunter-gatherers, directed the families of farmers, managed the assembly lines of industry. We even conceptualized the possibility of creating a new, computer-based "man," born of expert systems and reared in the artificial intelligence systems of the Electronics Era.

In the Information Age, information is "the Man." "The Man" brings its own meaning, carries its own ethics, dictates its own direction. We need only receive this information lovingly and process it systematically, and we will share in the excitement of birth and maturity, death and rebirth. As with the growth of productive information, we may grow forever.

It is certain that information is our life. To the extent we use our brains to process information, to that same extent do we ensure the building of potent, intense and enduring neurons which define human life—for now and evermore. To the degree that we use information to empower people to make free and productive choices in their lives, to that same degree do we facilitate the movement of civilization into a great new Age of Ideation.

References

Alexik, M. and Carkhuff, R. R. The Effects of the Manipulation of Client Depth of Self-Exploration upon High and Low Functioning Counselors. *Journal of Clinical Psychology,* 1967, *23,* 212–215.

Anthony, W. *The Principles of Psychiatric Rehabilitation.* Baltimore, MD: University Park Press, 1979.

Anthony, W. A Skills Training Approach in Psychiatric Rehabilitation. *Rehabilitation Brief,* 1980, *4,* No. 1.

Anthony, W. An Assessment of Frequency of the Usage of the Term, Skills, in the Helping Literature Prior to and Subsequent to Carkhuff's 1974 Keynote Address. Personal Communication, 1982.

Anthony, W., Buell, G. J., Sharratt, S. and Althoff, M.E. The Efficacy of Psychiatric Rehabilitation. *Psychological Bulletin,* 1972, *78,* 447–456.

Anthony, W., Cohen, M. and Pierce, R. *Instructor's Guide to the Psychiatric Rehabilitation Series.* Amherst, MA: Carkhuff Institute of Human Technology, 1979.

Anthony, W. and Drasgow, J. A Human Technology for Human Resource Development. *Counseling Psychologist,* 1978, *7,* 58–65.

Anthony, W., Pierce, R. and Cohen, M. *The Skills of Rehabilitation Programming.* Amherst, MA: Carkhuff Institute of Human Technology, 1979 (b).

Anthony, W. and Wain, H. J. Investigation of the Outcome of Empathy Training for Medical Corpsmen. *Psychological Aspects of Disability,* 1971, *18,* 86–88.

Aspy, D. N. The Effect of Teacher-Offered Conditions of Empathy, Consequence, and Positive Regard upon Student Achievement. *Florida Journal of Educational Research,* 1969, *11,* 39–48.

Aspy, D. N. Reaction to Carkhuff's Articles. *Counseling Psychologist,* 1972, *3,* 31–34 (a).

Aspy, D. N. *Toward a Technology for Humanizing Education.* Urbana, IL: Research Press, 1972 (b).

Aspy, D. N. Beyond Rhetoric. *Counseling Psychologist,* 1973, *4,* 108–110.

Aspy, D. N., Aspy, C. B. and Roebuck, F. N. *Third Century in American Education: International Conference on Productivity in Education.* Denton, TX: Texas Women's University, 1982.

Aspy, D. N. and Hadlock, W. The Effects of High and Low Functioning Teachers upon Student Performance. In Carkhuff, R. R. and Berenson, B. G., *Beyond Counseling and Therapy.* NY: Holt, Rinehart & Winston, 1967. Also in D. N. Aspy and F. N. Roebuck, *A Lever Long Enough.* Dallas, TX: National Consortium for Humanizing Education, 1976.

Aspy, D. N. and Roebuck, F. N. *KIDS Don't Learn from People They Don't Like.* Amherst, MA: HRD Press, Inc., 1977.

Aspy, D. N. and Roebuck, F. N. The Effects of the Principal's Interpersonal Skills upon Teacher Work Variables. *Research Reports, Carkhuff Institute of Human Technology,* 1978, *2,* No. 4.

Aspy, D. N. and Roebuck, F. N. Researching Person-Centered Issues in Education. In C. R. Rogers, *Freedom to Learn.* Boston, MA: Houghton Mifflin, 1983.

Authier, J. and Gustafson, K. *Enriching Intimacy.* Omaha, NB: University of Nebraska Medical Center, 1973.

Banks, G. *IPS-Based Inservice Teacher Education.* Seattle, WA: Washington Education Association, 1980.

Banks, G. and Anthony, W. The Helping Profession's Response to Carkhuff: A Choice for Adolescence or Adulthood. *Counseling Psychologist,* 1973, *4,* 102–108.

Banks, G., Benividez, P. and Bergeson, N. *The Training of Rural School Teachers in Interpersonal and Content Development Skills and Pupil Effects.* Seattle, WA: Washington Education Association, 1981.

Banks, G., Cannon, J. R., Carkhuff, R. R., Friel, T. W., McCune, S. and Pierce, R. M. Management Systems Designs in Government, Chapter 13 in R. R. Carkhuff, *Sources of Human Productivity.* Amherst, MA: HRD Press, Inc., 1983.

References

Barnet, J. Career Counseling Program Gives Residents Helpful Job-Seeking Hints. *Corrections in Illinois,* 1976, *3,* No. 4.

Barrett-Lennard, G. T. The Empathy Cycle: Refinement of a Nuclear Concept. *Journal of Counseling Psychology,* 1981, *28,* 91–100.

Battenschlag, J. Career Achievement Skills Delivery System. *Journal of Research and Development in Education,* 1974, *7,* No. 3.

Battenschlag, J., Ahearn, J., Burklow, M., Danley, K., Jeter, K., Landers, D., Phillips, L., Rochow, R., Safir, D. and Yausen, G. *Human and Computer Assisted Career Achievement Skills Training.* Pontiac, MI: Pontiac Public School District, 1974.

Bellingham, R. *The Effects of Interpersonal Skills Training for Elementary Teachers and Students.* Kalamazoo, MI: Kalamazoo Institute for Human Resource Development, 1978 (a).

Bellingham, R. On Researching the Researchers. *Counseling Psychologist,* 1978, *7,* 55–58 (b).

Bellingham, R. and Devine, J. *The Effects of HRD Training on Recidivism in a County Jail.* Kalamazoo, MI: Kalamazoo Institute for Human Resource Development, 1977 (a).

Bellingham, R. and Devine, J. *Helping People.* Kalamazoo, MI: Kalamazoo Institute for Human Resource Development, 1977 (b).

Bellingham, R. and Devine, J. *Assessment of Human Resource Development Skills.* Kalamazoo, MI: Kalamazoo Institute for Human Resource Development, 1978.

Bendix, L. *The Differential Effects on Parents and Their Children of Training Parents to be Helpers or Life Skill Trainers for Their Children.* Doctoral Dissertation, Boston University, 1977.

Benevidez, P., Banks, G. and Bergeson, N. *The Training of Urban School Teachers in Interpersonal and Content Development Skills and Pupil Effects.* Seattle, WA: Washington Educational Association, 1981.

Berenson, B. G. and Carkhuff, R. R. *Sources of Gain in Counseling and Psychotherapy.* NY: Holt, Rinehart & Winston, 1967.

Berenson, B. G., Carkhuff, R. R. and Myrus, P. The Interpersonal Functioning and Training of College Students. *Journal of Counseling Psychology,* 1966, *13,* 441–446.

Berenson, B. G. and Mitchell, K. *Confrontation.* Amherst, MA: HRD Press, Inc., 1974.

Berenson, D. H. The Effects of Systematic Human Relations Training upon Classroom Performance of Elementary School Teachers. *Journal of Research and Development in Education,* 1971, *4,* 70–86.

Berenson, D. H., Berenson, S. R., Berenson, B. G., Carkhuff, R. R., Griffin, A. H. and Ransom, B. M. The Physical, Emotional and Intellectual Effects of Teaching Learning Skills to Minority Group Drop-Out Learners. *Research Reports, Carkhuff Institute of Human Technology,* 1978, *2,* No. 1.

Berenson, D. H. and Savidge, D. *The Effects of IPS-Based Discipline Programs upon Student Discipline Problems.* Amherst, MA: Carkhuff Institute of Human Technology, 1981.

Bergeson, T. *IPS-Based Educational Leadership Training.* Seattle, WA: Washington Education Association, 1983.

Bergin, A. E. and Lambert, M. J. The Evaluation of Therapeutic Outcome. In S. L. Garfield and A. E. Bergin (Eds.), *Handbook of Psychotherapy and Behavior Change,* NY: Wiley, 1978.

Bierman, R., Davison, B., Finkelman, L., Leonidas, J., Lumley, C. and Simister, S. *Toward Meeting Fundamental Human Service Needs.* Guelph, Ontario: Human Service Community, Inc., 1976.

Bierman, R., Santilli, M. and Carkhuff, R. R. Efficacy of Empathic Communication Learning Groups for Inner-City Preschool Teachers and Family Workers. *Behavioral Sciences,* 1972, *8,* 188–202.

Blakeman, J. D. (Ed.). *Interpersonal Skills for Corrections: Conference Proceedings.* Washington, DC: National Institute of Corrections, 1980.

Blalock, C. and Aspy, D. N. The Effects of Interpersonal Skills upon the Amount of Information Obtained in a Medical Interview. *Research Reports, Carkhuff Institute of Human Technology,* 1979, *3,* No. 3.

Bloom, B. S., Englehart, M. D., Furst, E. J., Hill, W. H. and Krathwohl, D. R. *A Taxonomy of Educational Objectives: Handbook I, The Cognitive Domain.* NY: Longmons, Green, 1956.

References

Bopp, K., Bushee, K. and Chapados, J. *The Effects of HRD Skills Training Interventions in Developmental Functional Depression.* Duluth, MN: School of Education, University of Minnesota, 1978 (a).

Bopp, K., Bushee, K. and Chapados, J. *The Effect of a Human Technology Training Program in a Volunteer Crisis Intervention Center.* Duluth, MN: School of Education, University of Minnesota, 1978 (b).

Bopp, K. and Chapados, J. *The Outcomes of Life Skills Training Approach to Marital Counseling.* Duluth, MN: School of Education, University of Minnesota, 1978.

Bouie, V. and Chapados, J. *Training of Minority Career Counselors in Interpersonal Skills as an Adjunct to Career Development Skills Training.* Duluth, MN: School of Education, University of Minnesota, 1978.

Bozarth, J. D. and Rubin, S. E. Empirical Observations of Rehabilitation Counselor Performance and Outcome: Some Implications. *Rehabilitation Counseling Bulletin,* September, 1975, 294–298.

Brillinger, R. H. and Friel, T. W. *PRIDE Program at Northern Wood Preserves.* Toronto, Canada: Abitibi-Price, 1981. Also, Chapter 9 in R. R. Carkhuff, *Sources of Human Productivity.* Amherst, MA: HRD Press, Inc., 1983.

Bruh, M., Schwab, R. J. und Tausch, R. Die Auswirkungen inteusiver personenzentrieter Gesprachsgrupper bei Klienten und seelischer Beeintrachtigungen. *Aeitschrift für Klinische Psychologie.* 1980.

Bushee, K. and Chapados, J. *The Efficacy of Human Technology Skills Training as a Basis for a Parenting Program.* Duluth, MN: School of Education, University of Minnesota, 1978.

Bushee, K. and Chapados, J. *The Effects of Supervisory Interpersonal Skills Training.* Duluth, MN: School of Education, University of Minnesota, 1980.

Cabush, D. W. and Edwards, K. J. Training Clients to Help Themselves: Outcome Effects of Training College Student Clients in Facilitative Self-Responding. *Journal of Counseling Psychology,* 1976, *23,* 34–39.

Cannon, J. R. and Carkhuff, R. R. Effects of Rater Level of Functioning and Experience upon the Discrimination of Facilitative Conditions. *Journal of Consulting and Clinical Psychology,* 1969, *33,* 189–194.

Cannon, J. R. and Pierce, R. M. Order Effects in the Experimental Manipulation of Therapeutic Conditions. *Journal of Clinical Psychology,* 1968, *24,* 242–244.

Carkhuff, R. R. Training in Counseling and Psychotherapy: Requiem or Reveille? *Journal of Counseling Psychology,* 1966, *13,* 360–367.

Carkhuff, R. R. *Helping and Human Relations.* NY: Holt, Rinehart & Winston, 1969.

Carkhuff, R. R. *The Development of Human Resources.* NY: Holt, Rinehart & Winston, 1971 (a).

Carkhuff, R. R. Training as a Preferred Mode of Treatment. *Journal of Counseling Psychology,* 1971, *18,* 123–131 (b).

Carkhuff, R. R. The Development of Systematic Human Resource Development Models. *Counseling Psychologist,* 1972, *3,* 4–11 (a).

Carkhuff, R. R. New Directions in Training for the Helping Professions: Toward a Technology for Human and Community Resource Development. *Counseling Psychologist,* 1972, *3,* 12–30 (b).

Carkhuff, R. R. What's It All About Anyway? Some Reflections on Helping and Human Resource Development Models. *Counseling Psychologist,* 1972, *3,* 79–87 (c).

Carkhuff, R. R. *The Art of Problem-Solving.* Amherst, MA: HRD Press, Inc., 1973.

Carkhuff, R. R. *Promise of America.* New Orleans, LA: American Personnel and Guidance Association, 1974.

Carkhuff, R. R. *The Art of Program Development.* Amherst, MA: HRD Press, Inc., 1975.

Carkhuff, R. R. *Toward Actualizing Human Potential.* Amherst, MA: HRD Press, Inc., 1981.

Carkhuff, R. R. Affective Education in the Age of Productivity. *Journal of Educational Leadership,* 1982, *39,* 484–487 (a).

References

Carkhuff, R. R. Improving Human Performance. In C. R. Macdonald, *A Guide to Developing Outstanding Supervisors: An AT&T Study of Supervisory Performance.* Amherst, MA: HRD Press, Inc., 1982 (b).

Carkhuff, R. R. *The Art of Helping V.* Amherst, MA: HRD Press, Inc., 1983 (a).

Carkhuff, R. R. *Human Productivity.* Amherst, MA: HRD Press, Inc., 1983 (b).

Carkhuff, R. R. and Alexik, M. The Differential Effects of the Manipulation of Client Self-Exploration upon High and Low Functioning Therapists. *Journal of Counseling Psychology,* 1967, *14,* 350–355.

Carkhuff, R. R. and Banks, G. Training as a Preferred Mode of Facilitating Relations between Races and Generations. *Journal of Counseling Psychology,* 1970, *17,* 413–418.

Carkhuff, R. R. and Berenson, B. G. *Beyond Counseling and Therapy.* NY: Holt, Rinehart & Winston, 1967.

Carkhuff, R. R. and Berenson, B. G. *Teaching as Treatment.* Amherst, MA: HRD Press, Inc., 1976.

Carkhuff, R. R. and Berenson, B. G. *The Skilled Teacher.* Amherst, MA: HRD Press, Inc., 1981.

Carkhuff, R. R. and Bierman, R. Training as a Preferred Mode of Treatment of Parents of Emotionally Disturbed Children. *Journal of Counseling Psychology,* 1970, *17,* 157–161.

Carkhuff, R. R., Devine, J., Berenson, B. G., Griffin, A. H., et al. *Cry Twice!* Amherst, MA: HRD Press, Inc., 1974.

Carkhuff, R. R. and Friel, T. W. *The Art of Developing a Career.* Amherst, MA: HRD Press, Inc., 1974.

Carkhuff, R. R. and Friel, T. W. *The Efforts of IPS-Based Training upon Administrators.* Lansing, MI: Michigan Department of Education, 1974.

Carkhuff, R. R. and Griffin, A. H. The Development of Effective Courses of Action for Ghetto School Children. *Psychology in the Schools,* 1970, *7,* 272–274.

Carkhuff, R. R., Griffin, A. H. and Mallory, R. M. *The LEAST Approach to Classroom Discipline.* In National Education Association, *A Design for Discipline.* Washington, DC: NEA, 1978.

Carkhuff, R. R., Kratochvil, D. and Friel, T. Effects of Professional Training Communication and Discrimination of Facilitative Conditions. *Journal of Counseling Psychology,* 1968, *15,* 68–74.

Carkhuff, R. R. and Truax, C. B. Lay Mental Health Counseling: The Effects of Lay Group Counseling. *Journal of Consulting Psychology,* 1965, *29,* 426–431 (a).

Carkhuff, R. R. and Truax, C. B. Training in Counseling and Psychotherapy: An Evaluation of an Integrated Didactic and Experiential Approach. *Journal of Consulting Psychology,* 1965, *25,* 333–336 (b).

Carnavale, A. P. *Human Capital.* Washington, DC: ASTD, 1983.

Chapados, J. *The Efficacy of a Systematic HRD Skills Training Program for Detoxification Center Counselors.* Duluth, MN: School of Education, University of Minnesota, 1979 (a).

Chapados, J. *The Use of Human Resource Development Skills Training with Individuals Suffering from Chronic Behavior Disorders.* Duluth, MN: School of Education, University of Minnesota, 1979 (b).

Chapados, J. and Maloney, W. *The Effect of Interpersonal Skills Training upon Student School Behavior.* Duluth, MN: School of Education, University of Minnesota, 1978.

Chapados, J., Riehl, C. and Peterson, C. *The Efficacy of Conceptual Ordering Skills as a Treatment to Alleviate Thought Disorders.* Duluth, MN: School of Education, University of Minnesota, 1978.

Chingo, M. *Overview of Selected Offender Probation.* Kalamazoo, MI: Selected Offender Probation Office, 1978.

Cohen, M., Anthony, W., Pierce, R. M. and Spaniol, L. *The Skills of a Professional Evaluation.* Amherst, MA: Carkhuff Institute of Human Technology, 1979.

Cohen, M., Cashwell, A., Phillips, L., Holder, T., Cook, H., Ellis, O., Greenberg, B. and Renz, L. *Crisis Intervention in the Schools: What Happens When Teachers Ask for Help and Get It.* Youngstown, OH: Child and Adult Mental Health Center, 1976.

Cohen, M., Vitalo, R., Anthony, W. and Pierce, R. M. *The Skills of Community Service Coordination.* Amherst, MA: Carkhuff Institute of Human Technology, 1979.

References

Collingwood, T. *IPS and Aerobics-Based Teacher Improvement Training Programs.* Dallas, TX: Aerobics Center, 1982.

Collingwood, T., Douds, A., Williams, H. and Wilson, R. D. *Developing Youth Resources.* Amherst, MA: Carkhuff Institute of Human Technology, 1978.

Collingwood, T., Williams, H. and Douds, A. The HRD Approach to Police Diversion for Juvenile Offenders. *Personnel and Guidance Journal,* 1976, *54,* 435–437.

Cox, A. *The Cox Report on the American Corporation.* NY: Delacorte Press, 1982.

Danis, S., and Hauer, A. *Helping Skills.* NY: Behavioral Publications, 1973.

Danley, K. *Project STEP: Final Report.* Boston, MA: Trilateral Council for Quality Education, 1980.

Danley, K., Ahearn, J., and Battenschlag, J. *Learning Center Report.* Pontiac, MI: Pontiac School District, 1975.

Davison, B. W. Conflict Resolution Workshops. Chapter 8 in R. Bierman, et al. *Toward Meeting Fundamental Human Service Needs.* Guelph, Ontario: Human Service Community, Inc., 1976 (a).

Davison, B. W. Continued Self-Realization Workshop. Chapter 9 in R. Bierman, et al. *Toward Meeting Fundamental Human Service Needs.* Guelph, Ontario: Human Service Community, Inc., 1976 (b).

Davison, B. W. One-to-One Tutoring. Chapter 13 in R. Bierman, et al. *Toward Meeting Fundamental Human Service Needs.* Guelph, Ontario: Human Service Community, Inc., 1976 (c).

Davison, B. W. Vehicles for Need Fulfillment: Overall Process Change and Group Climate. Chapter 4 in R. Bierman, et al. *Toward Meeting Fundamental Human Service Needs.* Guelph, Ontario: Human Service Community, Inc., 1976 (d).

Day, S. R., Methany, D. B. and Megathlin, W. L. Facilitation Training Model for a Correctional Setting. *Georgia Journal of Corrections,* Winter, 1972.

Day, S. R., Methany, D. B. and Megathlin, W. L. Training Correcitonal Personnel in the Helping Skills. In J. D. Blakeman (Ed.), *Conference Proceedings: National Training Workshop for Master Trainers/Consultants in Interpersonal Skills for Corrections.* Atlanta, GA: National Institute for Corrections, 1980.

Devine, J. *Human Resource Development Training in the Kalamazoo County Jail.* Kalamazoo, MI: Kalamazoo Institute for Human Resource Development, 1976.

Devine, J. *Second Annual Report.* Kalamazoo, MI: Kalamazoo Institute for Human Resource Development, 1977.

Devine, J. and Bellingham, R. *Outcomes of Training.* Kalamazoo, MI: Kalamazoo Institute for Human Resource Development, 1978.

Devine, J., Bellingham, R., Essex, G. and Steinberg, H. *Child Care Unit—Year End Report.* Kalamazoo, MI: Kalamazoo County Juvenile Home, 1977.

Devine, J., Bellingham, R., Essex, G. and Steinberg, H. *HRD Training for Ex-Offenders.* Kalamazoo, MI: Kalamazoo Institute for Human Resource Development, 1981.

Document Development, Inc. *Quantitative Analysis of Spring 1979 Student Performance: Project STEP Trilateral Council for Quality Education.* Boston: Trilateral Council for Quality Education, 1979.

Douds, A. *The Effects of IPS-Trained Managers upon Worker Performance.* San Diego, CA: Convair Corp., 1982.

Dowling, T. H. and Frantz, T. T. The Influence of a Facilitative Relationship on Interactive Learning. *Journal of Counseling Psychology,* 1975, *22,* 259–264.

Drasgow, J. A. *Five Year Follow-Up of Group Therapy for Alcoholics.* Buffalo, NY: V.A. Hospital, 1981.

Egan, G. *The Skilled Helper.* Monteray, CA: Brooks-Cole, 1975.

Egloff, J. *The Effects of IPS-Trained Peer Tutors upon Slow Readers.* Flint, MI: Genesee Intermediate School District, 1972.

Evans, G. P. and Vitalo, R. *Helping Youths Succeed through Systematic HRD Intervention.* Youngstown, OH: Child and Adult Mental Health Center, 1976.

References

Farkas, M. D. *The Effects of Training Psychiatric Staff in Human Relations Skills: Developing a Rehabilitation Model for Chronic Patients During Deinstitutionalization.* Doctoral Dissertation, Boston University, 1980.

Feder, E. *Assessing IPS-Based Foundations of Management Training.* New Orleans, LA: AMOCO, Inc., 1982 (a).

Feder, E. *The Effects of IPS-Based Management Training.* New Orleans, LA: AMOCO, Inc., 1982 (b).

Finkelman, L. Changes in Need Fulfillment. Chapter 5 in R. Bierman, et al. *Toward Meeting Fundamental Human Service Needs.* Guelph, Ontario: Human Service Community, Inc., 1976.

Flanders, N. A. *Analyzing Teaching Behavior.* Reading, MA: Addison-Wesley, 1970.

Friel, T. W. *The Student's and Counselor's Guide to Career Decision-Making Skills.* Flint, MI: Genesee Intermediate School District, 1972.

Friel, T. W., Berenson, D. H., Pierce, R. M., Battenschlag, J. and Rochow, R. *The Effects of HRD Training upon Youth Career Development.* Flint, MI: Genesee Intermediate School District, 1974.

Friel, T. W., Drake, J., Tyler, N. and Mallory, A. E. The Development, Re-development and Human Resource Development Implications for the Computer-Based Guidance Program (ECES). *Michigan Personnel and Guidance Journal,* 1972, *4,* 10–24.

Friel, T. W., Franckowiak, B. and Holder, T. *The Effectiveness of Youth Employment Training Programs—Six Months Later.* Flint, MI: Genesee Intermediate School District, 1979.

Friel, T. W. and Holder, T. *An Evaluation of a Work Preparation Training Program: One Year Later.* Flint, MI: Genesee Intermediate School District, 1979.

Friel, T. W., Holder, T. and Franckowiak, B. Training Youth to Cope in School and at Work. *The Guidance Clinic,* 1980, *12,* No. 10. Also *Michigan Personnel and Guidance Journal,* 1979, *11,* 23–28.

Friel, T. W., Holder, T. and Mallory, A. E. *Training Youth in Career Planning Skills.* Flint, MI: Genesee Intermediate School District, 1979.

Friel, T. W., Kratochvil, D. and Carkhuff, R. R. The Effects of the Manipulation of Client Depth of Self Exploration upon Helpers of Different Training and Experience. *Journal of Clinical Psychology,* 1968, *24,* 247–249.

Friel, T. W., Mallory, A. and Holder, T. CETA Youth Learn Vocational Skills. *The Guidance Clinic,* 1980, *13,* No. 4.

Friel, T. W., Pierce, R. M., Cannon, J. R., Feder, E., Holder, B. T. and Shultz, J. The Effects of Performance Management Systems. Chapter 14 in R. R. Carkhuff, *Sources of Human Productivity.* Amherst, MA: HRD Press, Inc., 1983.

Gage, N. L. *The Scientific Basis of the Art of Teaching.* NY: Teachers College Press, 1977.

Garfield, S. L. and Bergin, A. E. Therapeutic Conditions and Outcome. *Journal of Abnormal Psychology,* 1971, *97,* 108–114 (a).

Garfield, S. L. and Bergin, A. E. (Eds.). *Handbook of Psychotherapy and Behavior Change.* NY: Wiley, 1971 (b), 1973, 1978.

Gazda, G. Systematic Human Relations Training in Teacher Preparation and In-Service Education. *Journal of Research and Development in Education,* 1971, *4,* 47–51.

Gazda, G. A Critique of Carkhuff's Articles. *Counseling Psychologist,* 1972, *3,* 35–41.

Gazda, G. *Human Relations Development.* Boston, MA: Allyn, 1973, (a).

Gazda, G. Reactions to the Models of Zifferblatt, Blocher and Wolleat, and Carkhuff. *Counseling Psychologist,* 1973, *4,* 116–118 (b).

Geary, J. and Chapados, J. *The Effects of Teacher Interpersonal Skills Training Outcomes upon School Discipline and Incidents of Drug Abuse.* Duluth, MN: School of Education, University of Minnesota, 1980.

Genther, R. W. and Sacuzzo, D. P. Accuracy of Perception of Psychotherapeutic Content as a Function of Observers' Level of Facilitation. *Journal of Clinical Psychology,* 1977, *3,* 517–519.

Gladstern, G. A. Empathy and Counseling Outcomes. *Counseling Psychologist,* 1977, *6,* 70–79.

Goldstein, A. *Structured Learning Therapy.* NY: Academic Press, 1973.

References

Gomes-Schwartz, B., Hadley, S. W. and Strupp, H. H. Individual Psychotherapy and Behavior Psychotherapy. *Annual Review of Psychology,* 1978, *29,* 435–471.

Gorbette, R. and Chapados, J. *The Effects of Systematic HRD-Trained Counselors upon Student Discipline.* Duluth, MN: School of Education, University of Minnesota, 1980.

Greenberg, B. and Vitalo, R. *Teaching as Treatment as a Preventative Mental Health Delivery Strategy with Schools.* Youngstown, OH: Adult and Child Mental Health Center, 1981.

Griffin, A. H. *IPS-Based Instructional and Professional Development.* Washington, D.C.: National Education Association, 1980.

Griffin, A. H. *IPS-Based Physical, Emotional and Intellectual Inservice Teacher Training: A Design.* Decatur, GA: Georgia Educational Association, 1982.

Griffin, A. H. and Carkhuff, R. R. Training as the Preferred Mode of Treatment in Reducing Behavior Problems of Youth and their Families. In R. R. Carkhuff and B. G. Berenson, *Teaching as Treatment.* Amherst, MA: HRD Press, Inc., 1976.

Griffin, G. Training as the Preferred Mode of Treatment in Reducing Recidivism and Drug Usage for Ex-Offenders. In R. R. Carkhuff and B. G. Berenson, *Teaching as Treatment.* Amherst, MA: HRD Press, Inc., 1976.

Gurman, A. S. The Patient's Perception of the Therapeutic Relationship. In A. S. Gurman and A. M. Razin (Eds.). *Effective Psychotherapy.* NY: Pergamon Press, 1977.

Hall, R. *Correctional Counseling Counts.* Washington, D.C.: U.S. Bureau of Prisons, 1970.

Hall, R. *Inmate Reports of Correctional Counseling Effectiveness.* Washington, D.C.: U.S. Bureau of Prisons, 1971 (a).

Hall, R. *Research Reports.* Washington, D.C.: U.S. Bureau of Prisons, 1971 (b).

Hall, R. *Research Reports.* Washington, D.C.: U.S. Bureau of Prisons, 1972.

Hall, R. *Research Reports.* Washington, D.C.: U.S. Bureau of Prisons, 1973.

Hall, R. *Comprehensive Skills Training—An Effective Alternative to Traditional Juvenile Correctional Institution Programs.* Mandan, ND: North Dakota State Industrial School, 1978 (a).

Hall, R. *A Study of the Physical, Emotional and Intellectual Effects upon Delinquents of Comprehensive HRD Training.* Mandan, ND: North Dakota State Industrial School, 1978 (b).

Hefele, T. J. The Effects of Systematic Human Relations Training upon Student Achievement. *Journal of Research and Development in Education,* 1971, *4,* 52–69.

Holder, J., Tausch, R. und Weber, A. Forderliche Dimensionen des Lehrerverhaltens und ihr Zusammenhang mit der Qualitat der Unterrichsberitrage der Schuler. Unpublished manuscript, 1976.

Holder, R. T. *Preparing for Working.* Flint, MI: Genesee Intermediate School District, 1979.

Holder, R. T. Job Finding and Career Planning. *Occupational Outlook Quarterly,* 1980, *24,* 28–31.

Holder, R. T. *Career Development.* Flint, MI: Genesee Intermediate School District, 1982.

Holder, B. T. *Managing Performance Improvement.* Anchorage, AK: ARCO Alaska, 1983.

Holder, T., Carkhuff, R. R. and Berenson, B. G. The Differential Effects of the Manipulation of Therapeutic Conditions Upon High and Low Functioning Clients. *Journal of Counseling Psychology,* 1967, *14,* 63–66.

Holder, T., Drasgow, J. and Pierce, R. M. Examiner Communication Level and Objective Test Performance. *Journal of Clinical Psychology,* 1970, *26,* 3.

Holder, T. and Friel, T. W. Designing and Implementing a Program to Prepare Youth for Work. *Secondary Education,* 1972, *20,* 19–28.

Holder, T., Friel, T. W. and Tyler, N. Training Economically Disadvantaged Youth to Plan Their Careers. *Thrust: The Journal for Employment and Training Professionals,* 1979, *1,* No. 4.

Holder, T. and Schultz, J. *Long-Term Follow-Up Results of Interpersonal Skills Training: A Confirmation of Extrapolated Results.* Fort Worth, TX: General Dynamics Corp., 1982.

References

Holder, T., Schultz, J., Feder, E., Pierce, R. M. and Friel, T. W. *The Performance Management System.* Fort Worth, TX: General Dynamics Corp., 1982.

Holder, T. and Tyler, N. Self-Placement Training in the Classroom. *Michigan Personnel and Guidance Journal,* 1978, *9,* 45–48.

Hurst, M. W. and Hefele, T. J. Systems Analysis and Human Resource Development: Extension and Perspective. *Counseling Psychologist,* 1973, *4,* 123–125.

Inman, G. and Harberts, R. *Implementation of the Occupational Cluster Concept: A Curriculum Tool for Improving Career Development and Preparation Education.* Battle Creek, MI: Calhoun Area Vocational Center, 1976.

Ivey, A. E. A Time for Action: Can Counseling Psychology Respond to Systematic Training Programs? *Counseling Psychologist,* 1972, *3,* 70–74.

Ivey, A. E. Counseling: The Innocent Profession. *Counseling Psychologist,* 1973, *4,* 111–115.

Ivey, A. and Authier, J. *Microcounseling.* Springfield, IL: Thomas, 1978.

Jeter, K., Phillips, M., Lewis, R., Landers, D., Phillips, L., King, D. and Porritt, M. *Pontiac Adult Learning System.* Pontiac, MI: Pontiac School District, 1975.

Johnson, E. *Career Counseling Program: Final Report.* Chicago, IL: Law-Enforcement Commission, 1977.

Joost, H. Forderliche Dimensionen des Lehreverhaltens in Zusammenhand mit Emotionalen und Kognitiven Prozessen bei Schuler. *Psychol. in Erz. u. Unterricht,* S. 1978, *25,* 69–94.

Jung, H. F. Cotton, S. I., Hume, K. and Emergy, C. W. *Staff Development Training Manual.* Brockton, MA: Teleoanalytic Society and Institute, 1976.

Kagan, N. Observations and Suggestions. *Counseling Psychologist,* 1972, *3,* 42–45.

Kagan, N. *Influencing Human Interaction.* Washington, DC: American Personnel and Guidance Association, 1975.

Keeling, T. *Evaluation Report on Title XX Training Program.* Farmington, CT: Tunxis Community College, 1979.

Kelly, J. *The Effects of IPS Training upon Word Processing Output.* White Plains, NY: IBM, 1983.

Kenney, J. The Effects of Teacher Training in Interpersonal Skills upon Disadvantaged Pupils. In D. N. Aspy, *Toward a Technology for Humanizing Education.* Champaign, IL: Research Press, 1972. Also in D. N. Aspy, *A Lever Long Enough.* Dallas, TX: National Consortium for Humanizing Education, 1976.

Klyne, P. Dimensionen des Leherverhaltens in ihrem Zusammenhang mit Vorgangen der Schuler, Unpublished maniscrupt, 1976.

Korn, C. and Korn, H. A letter to Dr. Carkhuff. *Counseling Psychologyst,* 1972, *3,* 55–59.

Kratochvil, D. Changes in Values and Interpersonal Functioning of Nurses in Training. *Counselor Education and Communication,* 1969, *8, 104*–107.

Kratochvil, D., Aspy, D. and Carkhuff, R. R. The Differential Effects of Absolute Level and Direction of Growth in Counselor Functioning upon Client Levels of Functioning. *Journal of Clinical Psychology,* 1967, *23,* 216–217.

Kratochvil, D., Carkhuff, R. R. and Berenson, B. G. Cumulative Effects of Parent- and Teacher-Offered Levels of Facilitative Conditions upon Indices of Student Physical, Emotional and Intellectual Functioning. *Journal of Educational Research,* 1969, *63,* 161–163.

Lambert, M. J. Therapist Interpersonal Skills and Their Relationship to Psychotherapy Outcome. In E. Marshall and D. Kurtz (Eds.), *Training in Interpersonal Skills.* In press, Brooks-Cole, 1983.

Lambert, M. J. and DeJulio, S. S. Outcome Research in Carkhuff's Human Resource Development Training Programs. *The Counseling Psychologist,* 1977, *6,* 79–86.

Lambert, M. J., DeJulio, S. S. and Stern, D. M. Therapist Interpersonal Skills: Process, Outcome, Methodological Considerations, and Recommendations for Future Research. *Psychological Bulletin,* 1978, *85,* 467–489.

References

Leonidas, J. The Adult-Child Workshop. Chapter 7 in R. Bierman, et al. *Toward Meeting Fundamental Human Service Needs.* Guelph, Ontario: Human Service Community, Inc., 1976, (a).

Leonidas, J. Delivering a Preventative Social Service in a Public School: Trained Community Volunteer Helpers Working with Vulnerable Public School Children. Chapter 15 in R. Bierman, et al. *Toward Meeting Fundamental Human Service Needs.* Guelph, Ontario: Human Service Community, Inc., 1976 (b).

Lumley, C. Basic Job Readiness Training Program. Chapter 14 in R. Bierman, et al. *Toward Meeting Fundamental Human Service Needs.* Guelph, Ontario: Human Service Community, Inc., 1976.

Mallory, A. E. and Battenschlag, J. *Teacher Training Project to Improve the Statewide Delivery of Adult Competencies.* Flint, MI: Genesee Intermediate School District, 1979

Mallory, R. M. The Teacher who Disciplines LEAST. *Today's Education,* April–May 1979, 23–26.

Maloney, W. and Chapados, J. *The Effects of Systematic Life Skills Training upon Problem Youth.* Duluth, MN: School of Education, University of Minnesota, 1978 (a).

Maloney, W. and Chapados, J. *The Use of Interpersonal Skills to Mediate Drug- and Alcohol-Induced Behavioral Crises.* Duluth, MN: School of Education, University of Minnesota, 1978 (b).

Marshall, E. and Kurtz, D. *Training in Interpersonal Skills.* Santa Clara: Brooks-Cole, 1982.

Martin, J. and Carkhuff, R. R. Changes in Personality and Interpersonal Functioning of Counselors-in-Training. *Journal of Clinical Psychology,* 1968, *24,* 109–110.

Matarazzo, R. G. Research on the Teaching and Learning of Psychotherapeutic Skills. In S. L. Garfield and A. E. Bergin (Eds.), *Handbook of Psychotherapy and Behavior Change.* NY: Wiley, 1978.

Megathlin, W. L. *The Effects of Facilitation Training Provided by Correctional Offices.* Washington, D.C.: U.S. Department of Justice, 1969 (a).

Megathlin, W. L. *Effects of Facilitation Training Provided by Correctional Offices: Follow-Up Report.* Washington, D.C.: U.S. Department of Justice, 1969 (b).

Megathlin, W. L. and Day, S. R. Effects of Facilitation Training on Correctional Personnel. *American Journal of Corrections,* April, 1972.

Mickelson, D. J. and Stevic, R. R. Differential Effects of Facilitative and Non-Facilitative Behavioral Counselors. *Journal of Counseling Psychology,* 1971, *18,* 314–219.

Middlebrooks, B. The Effects of Teacher Training in Interpersonal Skills upon Disadvantaged Black Youth. In D. N. Aspy and F. N. Roebuck, *A Lever Long Enough.* Dallas, TX: National Consortium for Humanizing Education, 1976.

Miller, H. and Berenson, D. H. *Occupational Cluster.* Battle Creek, MI: Calhoun Area Vocational Center, 1976.

Mitchell, K. M., Bozarth, J. D. and Krauft, C. C. A Reappraisal of the Therapeutic Effectiveness of Accurate Empathy, Non-Possessive Warmth, and Genuineness. In A. S. Gurman and A. M. Razin (Eds.), *Effective Psychotherapy: A Handbook of Research.* NY: Pergamon Press, 1977.

Montgomery, C. *Community Treatment Center Field Study.* Washington, D.C.: U.S. Federal Bureau of Prisons, 1977.

Morris, R. J. and Sucherman, K. R. The Importance of the Therapeutic Relationship in Systematic Desensitization. *Journal of Consulting and Clinical Psychology,* 1974, *42,* 148 (a).

Morris, R. J. and Sucherman, K. R. Therapist Warmth as a Factor in Automated Systematic Desensitization. *Journal of Consulting and Clinical Psychology,* 1974, *42,* 214–250 (b).

Morris, R. J. and Sucherman, K. R. Morris and Sucherman Reply. *Journal of Consulting and Clinical Psychology,* 1975, *43,* 585–586.

Mosher, R. and Sprinthall, N. Psychological Education. *Counseling Psychologist,* 1971, *2,* 3–82.

Mullins, T., Quirke, M. and Chapados, J. *Effects of Systematic HRD Training upon Organizational Task Completion.* Duluth, MN: School of Education, University of Minnesota, 1980.

References

Murphy, H. B. and Rowe, W. Effects of Counselor Facilitative Level on Client Suggestibility. *Journal of Counseling Psychology,* 1977, *24,* 6–9.

Myers, R. A., Thompson, A. S., Lindeman, R. H., Super, D. E., Patrick, T. A. and Friel, T. W. *Educational and Career Exploration System: Report of a Two-Year Field Trial.* NY: Teachers College, Columbia University, 1972.

Naisbett, J. *Megatrends.* NY: Warner, 1982.

National Education Association. *A Design for Discipline.* Washington, D.C.: N.E.A., 1978.

National Education Association. *N.E.A. Focus: Discipline.* Washington, D.C.: N.E.A., 1979.

Pagell, W., Carkhuff, R. R. and Berenson, B. G. The Predicted Differential Effects of the Level of Counselor Functioning upon the Level of Function of Outpatients. *Journal of Clinical Psychology,* 1967, *23,* 510–512.

Palau, J., Leitner, L., Drasgow, F. and Drasgow, J. Further Improvement Following Therapy. *Group Psychology and Psychodrama,* 1975, *27,* 42–47.

Parloff, M. B., Waskow, I. E. and Wolfe, B. E. Research on Therapist Variables in Relation to Process and Outcome. In S. K. Garfield and A. E. Bergin (Eds.), *Handbook of Psychotherapy and Behavior Change.* NY: Wiley, 1978.

Paul, G. L. and Lentz, R. R. *Psychosocial Treatment of Chronically Mentally Ill Patients.* Cambridge, MA: Harvard University Press, 1977.

Piaget, G., Berenson, B. G. and Carkhuff, R. R. The Differential Effects of the Manipulation of Therapeutic Conditions by High and Low Functioning Counselors upon High and Low Functioning Clients. *Journal of Consulting and Clinical Psychology,* 1967, *31,* 481–486.

Pierce, R. M. *The Performance Management System.* Fort Worth, TX: General Dynamics, 1982.

Pierce, R. M. Training in Basic Supervisor Skills: A Report on the Department of Education. In Chapter 7, R. R. Carkhuff, *Sources of Human Productivity.* Amherst, MA: HRD Press, Inc., 1983.

Pierce, R. M., Carkhuff, R. R. and Berenson, B. G. The Differential Effects of High and Low Functioning Counselors upon Counselors-in-Training. *Journal of Clinical Psychology,* 1967, *23,* 212–215.

Pierce, R. M., Cohen, M. R., Anthony, W. and Cohen, B. *The Skills of Career Placement.* Amherst, MA: Carkhuff Institute of Human Technology, 1979.

Pierce, R. M., Cohen, M. R., Anthony, W., Cohen, B. and Friel, T. W. *The Skills of Career Counseling.* Amherst, MA: Carkhuff Institute of Human Technology, 1979.

Pierce, R. M. and Drasgow, J. Teaching Facilitative Interpersonal Functioning to Psychiatric Patients. *Journal of Counseling Psychology,* 1969, *16,* 295–299.

Pierce, R. M. and Schauble, P. Graduate Training of Facilitative Counselors. *Journal of Counseling Psychology,* 1970, *17,* 210–215.

Pierce, R. M., Schauble, P. G. and Wilson, F. R. Employing Systematic Human Relations Training for Teaching Constructive Helper and Helpee Behavior in a Group Therapy Situation. *Journal of Research and Development in Education,* 1971, *4,* 97–109.

Pize-Kettner, U., Ahrbeck, B., Scheibel, B. und Tausch, A. Personenzen Trierte Gruppen und Einzelgesprache mit Psychisch Beeintracht-igten Hauptschulern aus 5.6 Klassen. *Zeitschrift fur Klinische Psychologie,* 1978, Band 7, Heft I, S. 28–40.

Rankin, R., Chapados, J. and Gorbette, R. *The Use of Interpersonal and Problem-Solving Skills Training to Enhance Roommate Compatibility.* Duluth, MN: School of Education, University of Minnesota, 1980.

Resnikoff, A. A Critique of the Human Resource Development Model. *Counseling Psychologist,* 1972, *3,* 46–55.

Resnikoff, A. Masters of the Ad-Hominem: Evaders of the issues. *Counseling Psychologist,* 1973, *4,* 119–120.

Rocha, L. The Effects of IPS-Based Staff Training upon School Productivity Indices. In D. N. Aspy, C. B. Aspy and F. N. Roebuck (Eds.). *Productivity in Education,* Denton, TX: Texas Women's University, 1982 (a).

References

Rocha, L. The Effects of IPS Staff Training upon Enrolling and Retaining Students in a Third-World Country. In D. N. Aspy, C. B. Aspy and F. N. Roebuck (Eds.). *Productivity in Education,* Denton, TX: Texas Women's University, 1982 (b).

Rocha, L. The Effects of Parent Training upon Child, Clinical and Parent Indices. In D. N. Aspy, C. B. Aspy and F. N. Roebuck (Eds.). *Productivity in Education,* Denton, TX: Texas Women's University, 1982 (c).

Rochow, R. *The Effects of a Comprehensive Intervention Program upon Latino Students.* Pontiac, MI: Pontiac Schools, 1982.

Rudolph, J. *Psychische Anderungen durch Gersprachipchotherapie und deren Bedingungen in her Sicht der Klienten.* Doctoral dissertation, University of Hamburg, Department of Psychology, 1975.

Rudolph, J., Langer, I. und Tausch, R. Prufung der psychischen Auswirkungen und Bedingungen von personenzentrierter Einzel-Psychotherapie. *Zeitschrift fur Klinische Psychologie, 1980,* 9, S, 23–33.

Santantonio, D., Brown, A. and Cohen, M. *From Crisis to Delivery: Rescuing a Child Care Curriculum Through the Introduction of HRD Skills Training.* Youngstown, OH: Child and Adult Mental Health Center, 1976.

Santantonio, D. and Vitalo, R. *Skills Training Approach to Resolving Mental Discord.* Youngstown, OH: Child and Adult Mental Health Center, 1977.

Scott, S., Warner, L., Powell, R. and Collingwood, T. *Youth Resource Development Training as Treatment for Juvenile Delinquents.* Dallas, TX: Youth Diversion Program, 1982.

Shores, M. and Vitalo, R. *Skills Training Approach to Resolving Mental Discord: A Replication.* Youngstown, OH: Child and Adult Mental Health Center, 1977 (a).

Shores, M. and Vitalo, R. *Teaching the Unteachable: The Impact of Teaching as Treatment Intervention with Severely Handicapped Children.* Youngstown, OH: Child and Adult Mental Health Center, 1977 (b).

Shultz, J. and Rowe, J. *An Assessment of Interpersonal Skills-Based Management Training.* San Diego, CA: Electronics Division, General Dynamics, 1982.

Simister, S. Community-Led Basic Workshops. Chapter 10 in R. Bierman, et al. *Toward Meeting Fundamental Human Service Needs.* Guelph, Ontario: Human Service Community, Inc., 1976 (a).

Simister, S. Community-Led Basic Workshops Compared with Staff-Led Basic Workshops. Chapter 11 in R. Bierman, et al. *Toward Meeting Fundamental Human Service Needs.* Guelph, Ontario: Human Service Community, Inc., 1976 (b).

Sprinthall, N. A. Human Resource Training: A Response. *Counseling Psychologist,* 1972, *3,* 56–61.

Sprinthall, N. A. and Erickson, V. L. The Systems Approach. *Counseling Psychologist,* 1973, *4,* 120–122.

Steinberg, H., Bellingham, R. and Devine, J. *The Effects of Systematic HRD Training upon Ex-offender Adjustment.* Kalamazoo, MI: Kalamazoo County Jail, 1981.

Stoffer, D. F. Investigation of Positive Behavioral Change as a Function of Genuineness, Non-Possessive Warmth, and Empathic Understanding. *Journal of Educational Research,* 1970, *63.*

Suchman, E. A. *Evaluative Research.* NY: Russell-Sage Foundation, 1967.

Tausch, A., Kettner, U., Steinbach, I. und Tonnies, S. E. Effekte Kindzenurierter Einzel-und Gruppengesprache mit Unter-Privilegierrten Kindergarten-und Grundachulkindern. *Psychol. in Erz. u. Unterricht,* S. 1973, *20,* Jg., 77–88.

Tausch, R., and Tausch, A. M. Verifying the Facilitative Dimensions in German Schools—Families—and with German Clients. Unpublished manuscript, 1980.

Tausch, A., Wittern, O. und Albus, J. Erzieher-Kind-Interaktionen in Einer Vorschul-Lernsituation im Kindergarten. *Psychol. in Erz. u. Unterricht,* S. 1976, *23,* Jg.

Theig, G., Steinbach, I. und Tausch, A. Schuler Fuhren Hilfreiche Gesprache mit Schulern. *Psychol. in Erz. u. Unterricht,* S. 1978, *25,* Jg., 75–81.

References

Truax, C. B. and Carkhuff, R. R. *Toward Effective Counseling and Psychotherapy.* Chicago: Aldine, 1967.

Truax, C. B., Leslie, G. R., Smith, F. W., Glenn, A. W. and Fisher, G. H. Empathy, Warmth and Genuineness and Progress in Vocational Rehabilitation. In Truax, C. B. and Carkhuff, R. R. *Toward Effective Counseling and Psychotherapy.* Chicago: Aldine, 1967.

Truax, C. B. and Mitchell, K. M. Research on Certain Therapist Interpersonal Skills in Relation to Process and Outcome. In A. E. Bergin and S. L. Garfield (Eds.), *Handbook of Psychotherapy and Behavior Change.* NY: Wiley, 1971.

Tyler, N. *The Effects of HRD Trained Counselors upon Community College Students.* Flint, MI: Genesee Community College, 1972.

Unger, K. V., Douds, A. and Pierce, R. M. A Behavior Curriculum: Skills Training Can Reduce Problems. *NASSP Bulletin,* September, 1979, 72–76 (a).

Unger, K. V., Douds, A. and Pierce, R. M. The LEAST Method of Discipline: A Research Perspective. *Research Reports, Carkhuff Institute of Human Technology,* 1979, *3,* No. 2 (b).

Valle, S. K. Alcoholism Counselor Interpersonal Functioning and Patient Outcome. *Journal of Studies on Alcohol,* 1981, *42,* 206–210.

Valle, S. K. and Marinelli, R. P. Training in Human Relations Skills as a Preferred Mode of Treatment for Married Couples. *Journal of Marriage and Family Counseling,* October, 1975, 359–365.

Vitalo, R. The Effects of Facilitative Interpersonal Functioning in a Conditioning Paradigm. *Journal of Counseling Psychology,* 1970, *17,* 141–144.

Vitalo, R. Teaching Improved Interpersonal Functioning as a Preferred Mode of Treatment. *Journal of Clinical Psychology,* 1971, *27,* 166–170.

Vitalo, R. *Improved Knowledge Acquisition Through Systematic Training of Student/Trainees in How to Learn in Groups: An Application of Teaching as Treatment to a Non-Distress but Dysfunctional Population.* Youngstown, OH: Child and Adult Mental Health Center, 1977.

Vitalo, R. *Four Year Analysis of Outpatient Deliveries.* Youngstown, OH: Child and Adult Mental Health Center, 1978.

Vitalo, R. *Report of Staff Training Services to the Prevention Program for Hispanic Families of the Multi-Social Service Center.* Springfield, MA: W. W. Johnson Life Center, 1981.

Vitalo, R. and Cohen, B. *Skills: An Effective Means of Delivering Outcome.* Youngstown, OH: Child and Adult Mental Health Center, 1976.

Vitalo, R. and Cohen, B. *Application of Teaching as Treatment Intervention to the Task of Improving Staff Use of Groups as a Service Modality.* Youngstown, OH: Child and Adult Mental Health Center, 1977.

Vitalo, R. and Ross, C. *The Differential Effects of Skills-Oriented Therapy and Chemotherapy with Chronically Mentally Ill.* Youngstown, OH: Child and Adult Mental Health Center, 1977.

Vitalo, R., Vitalo, P., Brown, A. and O'Donnell, P. *Teaching Counseling Skills Through Correspondence.* Thunder Bay, Ontario: Thunder Bay Mental Health Center, 1976.

Vitalo, R., Vitalo, P. Brown, A. and O'Donnell, P. *Effects on Clients of Therapist Training.* Youngstown, OH: Child and Adult Mental Health Center, 1977.

Wawrykow, G. The Effects of Four Models of Learning upon Learner Acquisition of Skills. *Research Reports, Carkhuff Institute of Human Technology,* 1978, *2,* No. 2.

Wiggins, J. D. A Comparison of Counselor Interview Responses and Helpee Behavioral Changes. *Counselor Education and Supervision,* 1978, *17,* 95–99.

Williams, H. and Barnet, J. Alberta Advanced Education and Manpower Correctional Officer Pre-Employment Training Program. Calgary, Alberta: *Alberta Solicitor General,* 1979.

The Human Sciences, Volume IV:
Interpersonal Skills and Human Productivity

The basic productivity systems themselves have changed in emphasis. Yet while human services are clearly in ascendancy over products as outputs, raw materials continue to dominate over information inputs; machinery supersedes the human mind of processing; and random sampling delays constant monitoring of results outputs and resource inputs as feedback. To sum, the productivity systems have not yet been dedicated to meeting human needs by maximizing results outputs and minimizing resource inputs.

In private and public sector organizations, leadership continues to be asserted by position rather than by the power of personal productivity. The organizations themselves are authoritarian and hierarchical while the greatest needs cry out for interdependency based on the complementary relationship of shared databases. The responsibilities continue to revolve around management rather than rely upon individual entrepreneurial initiative in little productivity centers throughout the organizations. Consequently, the relations are role-to-role rather than person-to-person and the dissemination of information is limited to the sparse data and response repertoires of a relatively few people. In short, the organizations remain the stolid, stone-age manifestations of Primitive Man rather than the dynamic, futuristic networking of truly Human Beings.

In turn, individuals have been retarded from becoming exemplary performers by continuing to emphasize their substantive specialties in single careers rather than developing core generic and supplementary skills in preparation for multiple careers. Relatedly, individual motives remain external-incentive-based rather than internal-actualization-based and their processing emphasizes conditioning rather than thinking. To summarize, our homes, schools, jobs, and communities continue to produce spinally conditioned, Industrial-Age performers rather than substantive informed thinkers.

In order to maximize the development of information, individuals and organizations are going to have to share data. The way that they share data is through the use of interpersonal skills. Each individual or unit or organization relates to the other individuals, units, or organizations by entering their frames of reference, seeing the world through their eyes, and communicating what they see. With this interpersonal communication, individual development and organizational productivity is possible. Without it, neither is possible.